To Mii
Your #1 To Me

love
Jan Sam

Book #3

Star Mentors Series

BECOMING THE IDOL

By Jay Jaworski

For my beautiful wife, Lisa
Without you nothing would be possible. You are my inspiration

Copyright ©2017: Jay Jaworski, StarMentors Publishing, LLC All rights reserved under international and Pan-American Copyright Conventions

Published in the United States by:
StarMentors Publishing LLC, Lakewood, Colorado

Inquires:
StarMentors Publishing LLC
P.O. Box 280724
Lakewood, Colorado 80228
CustomerService@StarmentorsPublishing.com
www.StarMentorsPublishing.com
www.BecomingTheIdol.com
800-773-3138

BOOK DESIGN BY: StarMentors Publishing LLC
Manufactured in the United States

FIRST EDITION

"Be the absolute best at what you do, be different, be the first to do it and be true to your art. Trust the wisdom and learn from the explorers who have taken the journey before you and never forget that this is the Entertainment Business. Your job is to entertain your way to success and transport others to amazing places."

Jay Jaworski

Introduction
For All Those who are Inspired to Shine – Let the Journey Begin

Thank you for taking the time to read Becoming the Idol. I am sure you will find my efforts untraditional and quite different than so many other music and entertainment industry books.

This book is NOT about "How" a particular artist made it to success. Instead it is about those behaviors, misconceptions, lack of perception, pitfalls and misunderstandings that prevent the majority of artists and bands from achieving the level of success that so many desire to obtain. This book is not a conventional approach, but an honest view into a different way of thinking.

The music and entertainment business is a very complex and murky universe and like the universe itself it has order, defined processes and constant forces that guide its component's interaction with everything else around it. All artists need to understand these forces and critical interactions at which to plan and predict a defined outcome of their efforts. This is not a throw it against the wall and see if it sticks business. Most do not know how to become part of the entertainment business family. This is essential to longevity, valuable relationships and prosperity.

For the select few that do establish a solid and thriving career in the entertainment business there are tens of thousands that don't get a chance to live their dreams or create long term successful careers. Many artists are wildly talented, true visionaries and gifted performers. In many cases, most artists deserve to be in a place where their art can be truly appreciated. The difficulty comes when their talent is improperly applied to build a vehicle that can be translated into something worth commercial value.

Most artists are happy being creators and players without journeying down the road of commercial existence but in my opinion, most artists want to achieve some level of success. This book helps lead the reader to understand some of the attributes that are misunderstood and expose critical behaviors that keeps someone from reaching their full potential. We all know someone who deserves to be on top of the world because they are unmistakably talented. We can also recognize behaviors in those same people that may be inhibiting their own chances to rise to success.

After 30 years in this business these behaviors continue to intrigue me. I have drawn my own conclusions and critical observations. This book carries its own weight in regards to shining a light on areas where an artist's perception can help change the outcome of their future. An artist has a choice to become successful or not. If an artist wants to be successful in this business, then the knowledge of what true "Entertainment Value" is and what the buying public requires is imperative.

Firstly, it is critical an artist must have purpose and a real goal. I ask you, are you any closer to your goals of career success than you were six months or two years ago? Can you actually measure it? Are you where you want to be? if not, then why? Are you getting ready to give up and find a new dream? Let's be honest with ourselves and assess our true intentions moving forward.

Are the "Dream Stealers" poisoning your chances of making it to the finish line?

As you read this book please take the time to reflect on how the information presented here can and if approached from a different perspective, can give you a new beginning or create a new direction to living your dream. This book may or may not be for you, but it is written from the heart. It was also written for my respect of all the talented dreamers in this world that I so much appreciate. If you do not agree with my intention and content of this book, then pass it along to someone that may embrace one simple approach that could change their life forever. Face it, you have to do something quite remarkable to make a mark in this business and shine. You deserve it, just like anyone else who has taken the journey before you. This book just might spark a new beginning for you.

Secondly, I wrote this book with great hopes for those who wish to go on a magical journey. I have tried hard not to just spill out another book on the same repetitive subject of making it in the music business wisdom regurgitation. I refuse to fill the pages with up-to-date music industry contact lists, legal subject matter or rehashed music business mumbo jumbo about contracts, promotional material creation and music submissions.

I will repetitively express my love for all artists and creative people who had that magic burned into their souls when they were born. These unique people have fascinated me since I was a young boy and this is still true today. Although becoming an accomplished musician, producer and manager myself, I have always been drawn to observing the moments in music that are truly magical. Everyone who loves live entertainment and live performance has experienced this magic. It all starts with anticipation that builds before the first note is played. The truth about live performance, if it is done right, most wish the show would never stop. A great live performance has the power to instantly turn audiences into lifetime loyal fans.

This art form is not just something that just happens, it is a reflection of the intent to create entertainment and everlasting memories by some very special people. This book is a simple effort to get the creative person who dreams all the time, all day and all night to want to be part of this magical industry. Each chapter presented is written to open fresh windows of thought, reflection, learning, opportunity and hope.

Most people never get a chance to reach or experience those dreams because of the infiltrators that show up to the party that I call, "Dream Stealers." "Dream Stealers" can be material, conscious, unconscious, normal obstacles of life or just a lack of focus, knowledge and dedication. Nevertheless, they can be toxic, poisonous and destructive if not carefully anticipated and timely acted upon. They can be a cancer that slowly erodes the energy and future of anyone that allows it to progress. Do you need an entertainment career health check-up?

This book will surely help the reader redeem their personal desires to make a mark in this business but it does take connecting with the essence of their own desires to land in a good place. No regrets, face the facts, only a few will make it to the very top but that is not the real reward. The most important thing is don't let anything steal your dreams or deter you from finding your true potential.

This book also explores the human journey to achieve a level of knowledge, creative expression and acceptance to participate in the entertainment process in one way or another. For some, the desire to become highly successful as a professional entertainer can be so overwhelming that every living moment is transfixed on this goal. This can either result in achieving the success one desires or blindly succumbing to the elements that can rob a very talented person of the opportunity to do what they feel they are born to do. Remember, "Dream Stealers" come in every shape, size and color. You should learn to become a doctor of "Dream Stealing-ology." The science can be unique to a specific artist, situation or environment. No matter how these obstacles can be defined they need to be understood, identified, realized, accepted and acted upon. Through focused gathering of the knowledge and tools needed for the journey, an artist can minimize the damage the "Dream Stealers" can have on one's ultimate goal.

In the real world, entertainment has since manifested itself into a completely limitless commercial industry. This industry is and continues to be built with the desire, dreams and ambitions of countless individuals to want to be part of it. The overwhelming desire to become successful in the entertainment business drives huge populations to compete in predictable ways. Why is that? This strong desire to "Live the Dream" takes on its own form that may or may not lead to a successful conclusion. This book also explores the key characteristics that are common to successful artists while focusing on the adverse and negative behaviors, actions and false perceptions that can produce the complete opposite desired results.

For the remainder of this book I will refer to these prevalent negative characteristics as the "Enemy of the Big Dreamer." Many say success is measured by how many high-level degrees one can obtain but in reality, many huge successes can be sprouted as a result of focused creativity, imagination, knowledge and a true purpose. I also hope to exposure significant factors that cut down the possibilities of failure in this business. I hope you find the content helpful and it opens your creative mind to a different perspective and approach to a very difficult but rewarding journey.

Therefore, before we get started and I take you on this journey, I must first ask you a few fundamental questions. I will be extremely honest with you while you read this book. You may question your own feelings and understanding of the music and entertainment industry but that is my objective.

Please take some time to really dig deep and think about yourself and the future you can change. Answer the following questions honestly:

1) Do you truly believe you have the talents and the unique abilities that are required to set forth a real career in this business?
2) Do you truly believe you have the creativity and artistic skills to create marketable entertainment value on a global scale?
3) Do you have the undeniable professional understanding and willingness to evolve and transform into a commercial level sensation?
4) Are you willing to accept the advice from the explorers and seasoned professionals that have taken the journey before you?
5) Are you willing to do all the things necessary to compete and become a true success in assuming the responsibility of the career you have chosen?
6) Do you have the right attitude towards the right values required to sustain and embrace the responsibilities necessary to make a life changing commitment within the music and entertainment industry?

7) Really, WHAT IS IN YOUR HEART?

If your answer is YES to each of these questions, then this book is for you. I will share with you a different prospective on the truth, mechanics and approaches that will guide you to your goal. Remember, this book is not about the "Established Super Stars" and how they "Made It" but it is about those who "Did Not Make It" and why. On the other hand, if you purely want to have fun with the music business or simply need a creative outlet then great, but if your desire is to become a leader and cement a long-term career then approach it as such. If you are NOT ready for the responsibility, then quit while you are ahead and take another career path and find something you have the burning desire and real purpose for. You must make the choice to either:

1. Build models of airplanes
2. Learn to fly small private airplanes or
3. Fly at incredible speeds in amazing hypersonic jets

There is a different kind of commitment to take anything to the third phase.

Success in the music and entertainment business is your choice. There is a process which doesn't happen by accident. Are you ready? Are you truly committed to take your career to the next level and take it to the "Third Phase?" Then let the show begin.

Become the "Next" Idol

Chapter 1
The Artist and the Entertainer Effect

There is nothing that has such a long history and endless future than the desire for people to be entertained or the desire to become a popular entertainer. Recorded history displayed within archeological artifacts provides a view into how entertainment has been a part of human nature since the beginning of time. The basic entertainment elements are expressed though art, dance or music or a combination of each. In addition, ever since the beginning of time there has been these unique people that today we call artists, rock stars and performers. Through a natural process these people have shaped the entertainment industry and the world we experience today.

The creative process continues to unfold perpetually taking differ forms, creative explorations and is ever evolving through cultural expressions. The evolution of the artist overtime has become a self-renewing resource. Each generation is unique but each continues to share common components and traits. Perhaps not when it comes to style and creative work but the common links has not changed much. Music and entertainment is burned into the very fabric of the hearts and souls of most people. One only needs to pay attention to the world around them to see how much music and entertainment is part of our daily lives. Even the birds communicate through song and performance. Young children are naturally fascinated by music, melodies and basic performance.

One can imagine ancient people gathering in a social environment responding to the sound of drums and primitive musical instruments made of bone, hides and wood. We can visualize ancient people dressed in colorful costumes that reflect their visual perception of their world and environment. We can visualize and almost hear the rhythms and sound that have a natural magnetic attraction and drawing effect on those within an ear shot of the event. What is unique even back then, there were a few special individuals (artists and performers) at the center of this phenomenon.

How effective would a movie, wedding, party or a social gathering be without music, dancing or other types of entertainment? Music and art is a universal phenomenon, it has no boundaries, no language barriers or rules. Only when intertwined with commercial business that we see measurable patterns and trends start to emerge.

I have spent considerable time traveling to modern and exotic counties to experience impromptu "Street" musicians and entertainers at work. My goal is to try to distinguish some of the basic attributes that artists possess that attract more audiences than others. Musicians and entertainers have been a part of this public spectacle in town squares and gathering places worldwide for eons. Certainly, the purpose of these artist's unsolicited performances are intentional to generate income for the musician or performer. However, I noted that for a few they just enjoyed being natural entertainers and enjoyed sharing their talent.

Many street performers I observed were not necessarily the most accomplished artists or very creative but they were able to bring in a few donations to make a small difference in their lives. Regardless, I caught myself observing some amazing artists that were wildly talented and accomplished. As you could clearly see, the donations they acquired were exponentially multiplied by the level and value of their performance. Time after time you would see a crowd of people surrounding a performer like a fortification wall. Each time there was something quite unique going on, something different, something unusual and something worth watching or listening to.

Now flash back a thousand years ago, where the same process played out when fire eaters, magicians, and musicians with a different sound, trick or instrument entertained the locals. The same process of turning audiences into fans continues naturally just as it does today. Really, nothing much has changed. I use this example because in its own little way, it's a reflection of today's commercial industry. This is a fundamental component that will always contribute positively towards the artist's future if they understand this basic principle.

As mentioned earlier, I keenly noted that the number of tips and donations placed into the street performer's (commonly called Buskers) hats, were multiplied many times over based on the quality of the performance. In some cases, the income was quite substantial allowing for a good consistent income. These were the true artists, weaving and executing purposed performances for their effect of financial gain and social acceptance.

I must purposely continue with this subject to clarify my point. On a few occasions, I went back and was mysteriously drawn to see the same spectacle unfold. These Buskers played their instruments and vocalized exquisitely. There was purpose in the intent. Perfection and amazement was their goal. They were giving the crowd what they wanted. They skillfully amazed total strangers and able to turn the unfamiliar audience into donators, tippers and fans. They knew how to use the power of entertainment value as their tools of the trade. Many onlookers took pictures, and video because they were amazed. Who are these performers? I had to buy their CD. They were true "artists" and were amazing. They did their job repeatedly to be able to realize the potential outcome of their efforts. They deserve everything coming to them, they understand the power of focusing on unselfish "Entertainment Value."

There is another side to the artist or group that does not have the same perspective or understand the concept of "The Power of Entertainment Value." This perception can cast a long shadow over a potentially successful career because of closed mindedness and isolation. A band of brothers and sisters that form a band together can call themselves artists while the fact is there may only be one or two cleaver creators in the bunch that drives the actual music or style that identifies the organization.

The act of trying to get all the individuals in a collective group to work, plan and evolve together can be extremely difficult. Although there may be some very talented individuals in the organization the group generally does not hold together long enough to "Cash In" on their efforts. Why is that? Like the accomplished street musician, the focus on the intent of the creative artist is what takes precedence over selfish desires. Do you want to create an academy award winning movie leaving a lasting impression or a B movie that stays in the theaters for one week? You do this by designing success at the beginning and then present it for the desired effect.

This focus has a cost. This process has been going on for centuries, not much has changed, and it is not going to change anytime soon. All the most popular well-designed works of art have outlasted time, while the imitations come and go and vaporize into oblivion.

To "Become the Idol" it is imperative that you put your best foot forward to become the best, the first or the most memorable no matter the process or cost.

Everyone is looking for the next hot thing, the new, the different, the best and the most entertaining. The artist who recognizes this can affect and change the direction of the outcome of their career. Later and throughout this book, I will expand on this subject and provide opportunities to explore the tools that all artists should deploy to get the desired effect from their effort.

The successful "stick to your ribs artist" takes action and puts forth an extreme effort. They want it and are willing to gather all the materials they need to build the bridge from dreams to reality. What effect do you want to have as an artist? Are you too cool for school or willing to deliver the goods through your focused intent?

Movie producers are masters of this behavior and construction. The bottom line between success and failure is a great script, a well thought out script, with a beginning, middle and end. Success comes from plugging in the right players to effectively deliver the goods. Musical artists are no different. It starts with great melodies, style or composition. The next steps are the players to effectively deliver the desired results. It is not unusual to listen to a good CD or album of songs to later see the live performance and be disappointed. While there are situations when the music is so well designed it does not matter at all that the players are not born to play live concerts and still sell millions of songs. It really does not matter except that designing the focus and creating the foundation for gaining the desired effect.

Many artists crank out marginal material just to have enough songs to play out. The commercial artist does not think that way. Each piece fits nicely together to create the overall effect to truly build entertainment value and facilitate the fans desire to "Follow" the artist. The artist must learn to become addictive to the music and entertainment lover. It does not matter what music style we are talking about. Everyone has his or her own style and the successful artist must navigate in that area to be effective or to last longer than a one-song hit.

Be the
"Stick to your ribs artist"

Chapter 2
Defining "Dream Stealing"

There are countless "Dream Stealers" and they fall into specifically defined buckets. Through my many years of dealing with countless musical artists spanning very diverse styles of the performing arts, age and gender, these pitfalls have become quite clear, identifiable and prevalent. Like any science, focused observation and time provide clues into this highly competitive world of no guarantees. Regardless of these pitfalls, some navigate by sacrificing time and sometimes their future financial security for an opportunity to take a shot at the golden ring.

This is not an isolated neurosis. This phenomenon is obvious with the current musical amateur competitions on network TV. Millions around the world watch attentively as hundreds of thousands of people withstand harsh elements just for a chance to get a taste of the commercial entertainment industry and "Become the Idol." We all have seen those who attempt to compete even though they know they cannot sing two notes in tune yet they are still compelled to put forth an effort. We all find this entertaining and in some cases amusing. To those individuals, the experience is both real and justified. To most, they could care less what others think about them but try anyway. I find this fascinating.

As an Artist Manager, this is a key element I look for when trying to select the right environment to invest my valuable time and efforts. I cautiously select which artist to work with. This also goes for the major music corporations, record companies, managers, agents and investors.

The complete belief in the dream of the journey and the destination truly is step number one and the cornerstone of success. Most can see it is not always the one with the best voice who wins but the one that is liked the most, entertaining and able to connect with the audience.

As I mentioned earlier, one of the first questions I need answered is: Is an artist willingly to obtain, learn or actually even possess the attributes, stamina and willingness to take sound advice? These major network competitions even bring in mentors to try to increase the chances that artists with potential can develop an edge to get to the next level.

The "Dream Stealers" are real and even the best can fall prey to the effects if the right focus and open-mindedness to new ideas and different approaches are not considered. There are rules and an order to the process and it should be understood. There is a side to you that can overcome the negative affects if common sense is applied.

"Dream Stealers" exist not just in the music industry but in every other high level of aspiration that one would desire to uptake. Think about it, if you wanted to climb to the top of Mt. Everest, build a multi-national manufacturing company or, command a space mission to mars, your acquired skills and knowledge are what will carry you to your destination. The difference with the music and entertainment industry is: One must be able to acquire the knowledge then invent or reinvent oneself into something of true entertainment value.

Really, where can a young budding artist get this information? This process is not a subject taught in school and generally it's a trial and error experience. It is remarkable how many millions of people desire to take this journey without any formal training or seek formal training programs to acquire the proper skills and industry secrets. No matter how someone tries to define success in the music or entertainment industry one must first know how to create or maintain entertainment value long enough to reach the level of success one desires in his or her dreams.

If an artist is to become either an internationally recognized recording artist or a locally recognized performer, both require a different set of rules, actions, sacrifices, behaviors, planning, engineering, commitments and compromises. Budding artists need to be smart and plan each step accordingly. One of the top "Dream Stealers" in the entertainment industry is: The failure to and unwillingness to conform, adjust and compromise to the current conditions of the market. Based on my vast experiences in the industry, many of the most talented individuals I have met over the years have ended up in the bottom of the abyss because of this simple misunderstanding.

Much like mountain climbing, if faced with an obstacle you must accept it and then engineer the means to overcome it. The music and entertainment business is no different. Most artists are typically so head strong and overly confident that they forge on to try to prove they are immortal and deserving of respect. They therefore don't follow sound proven advice or the established rules. Most of these promising individuals or groups fall into the pit of despair never to be seen again.

The truth is, artists are strange creatures and there is something a bit mysterious about them. They have a tinge of daredevil in them which is not a bad thing. It always amazes me to learn more about the endless creativity and how they utilize their talents to invent magic while at the same time destroy and systematically unknowingly dismantle their own futures.

In today's technological world, news travels at light speed. The desire to go viral outweighs the standard of the natural path of being discovered through the foundation building process in the real world. This is the future and artists are lining up to learn the hard lessons of this reality. The lesson is that the fundamentals of the entertainment industry still stands with a direct connection between people, performing live and turning audiences into fans "one fan at a time." Not understanding this basic principle certainly moves this fundamental mistake to the top of the "Dream Stealer" list.

"The Power of Entertainment Value, use it"

Chapter 3
Nurturing the Seed of the Entertainer

Before the days of internet, television, movies and cellular phones, the entertainment industry was fueled by its own basic principles of existence. Not much has changed when it comes to the desire to entertain others. Pick any time in history and you will always be able to find stories and references to famous musicians, history setting concerts and stage performances. As discussed earlier, the natural human desire is to seek entertainment while at the same time many desire to be the great entertainers. The same process exists. The human desire to be entertained will never change.

This is evident when watching a young child responding to smiling, music, animals and parents attempting to gain the child's attention. At the beginning, all children are exposed to natural performances by the "Parent Entertainer." In this technological world, parents try whatever means possible to entertain and occupy the child's attention using the hottest new electronic audio and visual devices. However, the first exposure comes through direct parental eye contact with the youngster and parental vocal inflections that peak awareness, such as singing. Some children start showing early signs of their awareness of their effects on others through their own simple performances that gains them attention. The birth of a creative artist is natural. This is the beginning of the emergence of a creative entity, and performer. Mix this with imagination, dreaming and inspiration and the rest is history. Development of an artist can start very early in life if nurtured properly in an environment that allows these skills to emerge.

If one pays close attention to young children at play, there is always one that is a natural performer or one with a vivid and expressive imagination. This occurs either naturally or through positive encouragement and reinforcement. The seed of the next superstar is there and sometimes hidden that needs some watering, a mentor, coach or career partner. This can also be true with a struggling yet talented artist perhaps even later in life.

Let's talk about critique and criticism of an artist. There is a strong difference between critique and criticism. Most artists cannot distinguish between the two. Young artists simply don't care what others think. They perform and express themselves naturally until the pain of criticism is felt and realized. This is the breaking point for most creative people. They either accept the pain or lose the spark and move on to something else in life. The ones that survive this early phase of overcoming adversity have a self-belief inbred that sets the cornerstone for a true creative artist to emerge. The true artist should and usually does seek honest critique and adjusts accordingly.

To excel and become a true entertainer one must simply love what they do, feel they are destined to be a success and be willing to enter the jungle and face the unknown. For all artists struggling to emerge through the smoke they must reflect on the fundamental aspect of the development phase and have a light heart about it. This business is about having a child like approach to things with the curiosity for the unknown. The journey is supposed to be fun and uncomplicated. Most make the process difficult and filled with drama and senseless wasteful efforts to even enjoy the journey itself. Most artists and bands have the seeds of success buried in them. Those seeds just need to be planted in the right soil and nurtured the right way. If the artist's seeds are not nurtured with the right nutrients, not given the right exposure to the spotlight and not regularly watered with pure entertainment intent then the seedlings dry up and wither away. Don't let that happened to you. To reap the harvest, the efforts are difficult and success is only realized based on the knowledge one needs to complete all the steps. Let your fruit ripen before you pick it. Don't get to anxious because you are hungry. Don't miss the best part of the journey.

Chapter 4
A Recording Studio in Everyone's Home

The music and entertainment industry and creative process was given a mega boost with the accessibility of affordable recording equipment, computers and integrated instruments. The digital era, advances in manufacturing, internet and accessibility to powerful and affordable computerized recording systems and electronics has ushered in a new age.

It is an exciting time for the creative artist located anywhere in the world to explore, create, produce and distribute their art. It has not always been so simple. In years past, it would take every dime an independent young artist or band made to record a handful of tracks. Not to mention the extreme cost to package and distribute their finished material. That is why the major recording companies existed, they alone possessed the resources to complete the process. Even the process of teaching young students about the entertainment and music paths has changed dramatically.

It is hard to find any form of quality music program in public schools today. Especially early in an artist's life due to funding constraints and lack of seasoned successful knowledgeable music teachers and dedicated mentors. In the past, music was an important subject, but today music takes a back seat to the hugely funded sports programs. Additionally, there has never been a place to learn about the basic mechanics of the commercial entertainment industry leaving inspired new talents to fly by the seat of their pants into the unknown murky world of the business. Don't fool yourself, all artists need to educate themselves about how the industry functions.

Where are the inspired artists of the world to learn how to navigate their way to a successful career in the entertainment business without proper guidance? Today this knowledge is at the tip of their fingers. Perhaps just like the way you might have found this book on an internet search.

One thing that has changed the face of the industry is the availability of affordable musical instruments, affordable computer recording software and point of creation digital file distribution access. Let's not forget the superpower of social media. Unlike today, musical instruments were expensive. It would have taken a king's ransom to outfit a performing group with the tools they needed. Today's costs is 10% of what it was 15 or 20 years ago. This accessibility and affordability has caused an explosion in the number of artists and bands that are formed each year. The side effect is a comparative increase in the competition for the "next best thing." This phenomenon also resulted in millions of new songs and video projects being created each year.

The competition is overwhelming and the buying audience has countless choices at which to spend their entertainment budgets. How does an artist get an edge against the competition? The answer is knowledge, creativity and understanding the battlefield. This is not taught in school, it is a learned talent unless a committed mentor or coach is made part of the equation. Another dilemma in our modern educational institutions is most schools don't even have quality instruments or teachers to teach inspiring artist and student show to play. At the same time new stadiums are built and huge school budgets are spent on sports and countless sporting events. This is why most musical artists venture on their own into the world of creativity and take the lone wolf approach.

Why are there not subjects such as Country Band 101 or Electronic Music Production 101, Artistic Marketing or Beginning Digital Recording offered? Certainly College level degrees can be obtained in these subjects but the artist birth process starts much earlier in life than that. If one examines the music and entertainment industry it is clear that music touches everyone, young or old. It is a huge worldwide industry and is in fact a real career path choice.

Ten of thousands of people venture onto the paths of this business each year. When students in today's schools graduate high school as adults they leave school not even knowing how to fill out an EZ tax form. This is a fundamental task that will be required throughout their life. That is because filling out a tax form is not considered important educational sanctioned power food. This makes no sense. The inspiring artist of today needs to have access early to the power food of the music entertainment industry to learn the right approaches, techniques, processes and qualification steps to become successful in their chosen entertainment career path.

No one can know exactly how many recording artists, inspiring musicians, songwriters and performers there are in the world. My guess would be in the millions. Also, because of time itself, every year there are millions more jockeying for their chance to de-throne the latest and most popular top bands or artists. The cycle of new acts and artists is a renewable resource ever expanding and never ending. Each year tens of thousands of budding inspiring artists are born or come of age. Each year countless artists who have worked diligently for years revisit their dreams and forge on to fulfill their goal of finally breaking though. Some of these individuals and groups are lucky enough to meet one another and magically combine into rarities that "Make It" to the "Big Time." Why, because they have something very special in the eyes of sponsors, advertisers, commercial entities, fans and records companies. The limiting factor is usually determined by "popularity and uniqueness." It is possible to become popular because of one performance on national television, a viral video, or a focused publicity stunt or just having created something with "True Entertainment Value." Nevertheless, there is only room for those who desire this level of success and what a small club it really is.

Let's take this into consideration, one in one hundred thousand perhaps gets the opportunity to do it as a sustained career. How do you increase your chances? The next few chapters will provide you with the key ingredients you need in your tool box. What can you build if your tool box only has a screw driver in it? What if your tool box included a saw, drill, hammer, a level and some nails? Your possibilities are endless? With a computer, sound editing software, proper plug-ins, microphone, integrated instruments and a little bit of creativity you can be one step away from your vision and dream.

> "The limiting factor is usually determined by popularity and uniqueness"

Chapter 5
Changing your Skin for Success

Many original artists make one grand mistake, believing they can please everyone. It amazes me what answers I get when I ask the question, "what kind of artist are you?" The majority say they can play all kinds of styles having a breadth of their talent that touch many different people. In reality, this response is the "Commercial Death Rattle." Your brand, focus and marketability dictate if and how you are to survive the first leg of the music business journey.

I would like to share an example of a life changing experience for a group of amazing players a few years ago in the LA club scene. This band was very popular, played all the top clubs, were in good demand and had an above average following. Each member of this band made a good living playing Hollywood clubs doing what they enjoyed. One year at Halloween, a club owner required that all the bands that were booked for the night dress up in costumes. All the booked bands accepted the challenge and dressed up into all kinds of goulash, scary and a hog-podge of characters. Some were quite inventive and clever.

This one band asked their girlfriends to dress them up as sexy girl rockers. They went way out of their way and did a great job with their look. When they appeared on stage playing their flawless music they were a knock out hit. I saw it for myself. Just because of the detail, effort, continuity and intent they created something that was different. They changed as performers and played it to the T, obviously having fun doing it. The audience clearly sensed it and played along. The visual spectacle they created resulted in the band being booked solid night after night, club after club, nationally and internationally. They became quite a success and made a fortune dressed as girl rockers. They went with it, did not fight it and adopted what was working for them. They discovered "True Entertainment Value" and it worked for them. This example is an extreme situation but the basic principle of creating value does not change.

A performing group or artist needs to take a real look at themselves. Surely the music is the engine and vehicle but the outside performance and clever branding is the flash that makes the difference. You can take a car and remove the engine and the mechanics that makes the vehicle functional but if the outside is attractive, well presented, nicely maintained, stylish and visually pleasing it sends a positive message. The music and entertainment business is focused on exploiting your primary senses of hearing and sight. Therefore, one without the other can limit one's chances of making the impression that one needs to survive in this business. That is why everyone going to a major concert are purposely dazzled by 20000 watts of lighting, smoke, and sound by the stage producers. Talented sound engineers focus and blend the audio performance elements for maximum affect and quality. Together all is designed for maximum affect and to create an audio/visual experience.

Artists and bands need to learn and excel in this thinking process to make the impressions that last. I will be brutally honest here. In my career I have watched thousands of bands and artists trying to make a lasting impression on an audience, the majority failing miserably. This is primarily due to inexperience and lack of understanding of what is expected of them as an artist. Believe it or not, those that wish to make it in this business have a responsibility to the audience to give them their monies worth. This lack of affect is not because their musicianship was not good but because the audience in most cases could not differentiate one band from another in style, visual impact or uniqueness. Generally, these are the same old doldrums of the same similar music with different players, the same look and the same old boring live performance. Who wants to see an inspiring magician that continues to use the same old trick of sawing a girl in half or pulling a rabbit out of a hat? They need to explore new and fresh new illusions to create value and interest.

Most bands and many artists do the same thing with their stage shows, music and overall presence and style. They also don't explore their own uniqueness but rather try to imitate other successful organizations. There is a bit of trial and error in the process but riding the coat tails of someone else does not create greatness. This is acceptable if the goal is to adopt the cover band approach. Some also think they need to perform countless already cliché' actions to qualify themselves as a bonified talent. A magician that engineers illusions that have never been seen, tried or performed and takes the time to make sure each effect is spectacular and amazing can create an entire international career out of only twelve illusions. The same perception can be compared with musical artists and bands. Twelve brilliantly written and engineered tracks with a flawless presentation visually and musically can win more fans than the street clothes band that has 200 hundred songs playing to the same old local following night after night.

Life changing performances should be designed from the beginning to be international in scope. Evolve into something new, exciting and marketable. What is wrong with moving from the comfort zone and change your skin. It is amazing how one's perception is changed about that old rusty car when it shows up with a new paint job, upholstery and new tires and rims even without changing the internal mechanics. What is magical is when the internal mechanics are also modified accordingly to complement the exterior presentation. It can change the artist or band in ways that are nothing but beneficial and rewarding.

How do you feel when you put on that new tuxedo or put on that hot new party dress? It almost feels like a super hero costume. It makes you feel good, it makes you act differently. It changes you but at the same time quickly changes your perception of yourself and everyone else around you. What kind of skin do you want to put on in regards to your entertainment career to stimulate the same affect?

Many artists have exemplary college level degrees in music. They may have countless years of musical evolution to understand every note, rhythm or composition but if there is no imagination and creativity there is nothing new to be brought to light. Just going through the motions does not create a true connection with the buying audience. As a mentor, my job is to encourage talented individuals to focus on their creative abilities using the building blocks of their knowledge base. A clever artist with focused and deliberate creative juices can write a multi-platinum melody with only three notes or three simple cords. Simply, if the artist cannot connect with the buying audience and evolve with the audience the success time clock starts running backwards. Not to mention the internal relationships of their organizations begin to degrade and the spark starts to diminish. All great relationships find ways to evolve and explore new levels and experiences. If something is not working for you change it. Don't be afraid. The audience is also changing right along with you. Accept it.

Chapter 6
You Never Know Who Is in the Audience

If there is one powerful lesson to be learned that will never change in the music and entertainment industry and sets the stage for disappointment it's: "You never know who is in the audience." Any artist that believes that they can drive their career from their sofa might as well go to trade school or college and hang up the big dream of being a successful performing artist. The road to success is paved with only the material that turns audiences into fans and hard work. Sure, there are flukes where luck paid dividends to a few individuals, but for the majority it is about "if you've got it, you've got it" and "if you don't, you don't." This is only proven in the battle fields of the public forum. If the audience likes you they will let you know loud and clear.

There are two very important facts that all budding artists must contemplate. One, believing that just because you upload your "amazing" music or "contrived" video to the internet it will explode like wild fire and make you famous. Two, this goes the same for those who shotgun CD's or digital files and EPKs to every person they can find on the who's who lists. Disappointment comes quickly with the hopes that these actions are going to facilitate a phone call offering a major record deal. The reality is in 99.9 % of these cases success just does not happen that way.

In today's worldwide major television talent competitions the following happens time after time: An 8, 10, 15, or 25 year old amateur bedroom performer takes the opportunity and signs up to compete. In most these cases, the competitor has never performed in public. But one amazing innocent performance in front of an influential judge and worldwide audience and it changes their life forever. Most bands and artists are in it for the fame and fortune instead of the opportunity of the humble expression of their art and talent. It is a natural process that should be allowed to open like a flower when it is time. It can't be forced.

The following discussion shall be directed at those who are to "Cool for School."

Any artist that thinks they are made of the right stuff certainly has a good start. There is nothing wrong with believing you've "got it," but your worth in the business can only be measured by the correct response from the audiences you place yourselves in front of. I have more respect for the street musician who in their own way understands the basics for success then someone with blind musical ambitions. The humble player would rather just play anywhere for anyone, not expecting anything except following through and just being a great entertainer.

To make my point a bit clearer, I have been acquainted with a reasonably good guitarist/singer who has made millions as a street performer by selling hundreds of thousands of CDs to passerby's. He is not the best singer in the world but has learned the process of creating meaningful and effective entertainment that sticks to your ribs, even if on a street corner. His performances are so memorable that he can draw you in and sell you a CD or just about anyone who stops by to watch him for 10 minutes. His other secret is he would rather sell a CD for $6.00 than for $15.00 dollars (he produced the original CD master for $500.00 dollars) so everyone can buy one. There is nothing wrong with a huge return on investment from selling music inexpensively, especially in these times. Not to mention, he also collects email addresses to add to his mountainous pile of international contacts to send great little videos to his "New Fans."

He plays in the same location seven days a week. He should be given a platinum record for his accomplishment. In the real world, if a record company is involved with an artist the artist would be lucky to receive a 15 % royalty. Not to mention the massive deductions by the record company which does not leave much for the artist at the end of the day. In this digital delivery world, pure profit making thinking is the fuel for future career development and sustainability.

When you go fishing for new fans you need the right bait and know how to set the hook. The commercial music industry is no different. Your job is to attract a promising sustainable future, attract the big fish, hook them and break the world record by landing the gold record. Your future will be struck during that one performance that one night when it all comes together. But you must be in front of the audience all the time to be at the right place at the right time.

Today your audience can be at the other end of a smart phone, computer or tablet. Don't assume what you are doing is working unless you can assess, measure and trend your effect on your audience. The "Dream Stealer" here is "assuming" what you are doing is working unless you can measure your affect and growth. Going through the motions does not count. If you design your process correctly, you should be able to assess and change your course quickly. Don't waste the audience's time with marginal material and performance. Wasting the audiences time is a triple waste of your time. You must see the affect, response, action and returns to be on course.

It is imperative to make quick simple frequent adjustments to make it to the destination. The market and buying audience is not stupid and they don't like being fooled. Your efforts in providing entertainment must be a real, deliberate, unselfish and honest effort. Look what happens to a huge performing artist who toured extensively to becomes a stellar success until the lip sync machine malfunctioned. Don't ever let your audience down. Always give them what they want and deserve. You never know when that magical moment will happen when someone in the audience who truly can change your life is there. You must hook the big fish and once you do they will invest their time, influence and money into your future.

There is not a better complement then "I am a fan." If your process and plan requires this behavior from your audience, then execute your best creation flawlessly. Only then will your efforts become life changing. When you have it right they will come to you.

"You never know who is in the audience"

Chapter 7
Creating "Entertainment Value"

Throughout this book, you will note I will refer to the term "Entertainment Value." many times. Regardless how each unique one of a kind artist tries to interpret this fundamental building block, most fall short in how to utilize its power. Artists must do whatever necessary to assure better odds of success in this highly competitive business. Simply put, "Entertainment Value" is the substance that the fans or audience take home with them either in material form or imbedded in their minds, hearts and souls.

Entertainment Value can start from just a simple poster of an upcoming concert, the quality of a recording, well designed lyrical hook, or how a production or concert is designed to unfold. Entertainment value is designed for cause and effect and to leave a lasting positive impression. True entertainment value powerfully affect audiences and activates the buying response.

As an example, if you were to receive a CD or digital music file from an unknown artist to listen to or review, how would you evaluate it? What are you expecting? You want to be blown away, Right? If it is over the top great then you become an instant fan. Giving respect to the artist, it is natural to have an expectation of some sort of openness to its content. Therefore, you prepare yourself, open your mind and in most cases are delighted to give the opportunity a fair shot. What if the recording was so badly presented and recorded that the moment sours for you? How can this situation have any value to you or the artist? I am sure if the opportunity came by a second time to review the same artist's work you would pass. There is a talent to this thinking process of creating a lasting and solid impression. This occurs during live performance as well.

Everyone has experienced a bad comedian, magician, singer, opening act or band. Sometimes it is almost painful to watch. The poison pill is where you or others have paid hard earned money to be utterly disappointed and feel ripped off. How can there be value in entertainment if it is not designed from the beginning to be successful? Don't do this to yourself. Take your time and do it right from the beginning. This is not a trial and error business.

Great movie scripts, sitcoms, stage shows and soundtracks are designed to have a predetermined affect in delivery and content. Most artists don't understand or have respect for the potential audience. Great designed entertainment value can make fans out of first time audiences and gain long lasting support. The fact is, most people want to become fans and followers of great performers, singers, musicians or unique bands. Being the same old thing just does not have or hold the support system up long enough to gain or create a sustained career. Don't go there, don't read that book!

Now that we have a better appreciation for the power of the development of "Value" in our efforts, we must now move forward. Keep this in mind and ask yourself, how can I create something really entertaining? How can I create something people want to see or hear again and again? It is essential you must work it out. Work with people who are good at these skills and who are good for your future. It is the entertainment business and the big stage we are talking about here. Actors learn to be actors that are memorable and singers, musicians, players and bands need to learn the same thing. You can't do it halfway, you must be "All In."

"You Must Create Entertainment Value"

Chapter 8
Put Your Shine On

For those who are interested in understanding what an Entertainment Manager's role is in the music and entertainment industry the following should be understood and interesting.

I receive countless phone calls from artists and bands seeking a Manager. It amazes me how the Manager's (Mentor's) role in the music business is misunderstood. Since this book was written by a Manager/Producer one needs to understand where this knowledge in drawn from that I share in this book. It is imperative that the knowledge being shared here should be linked to the fundamentals of the working requirements of a successful commercial effort.

A manager's job is not to secure employment for an artist or introduce them to commercial interests. Let's face the music here, a manager's sole responsibility is to advise, consult and help prepare the artist for the future. The following is the fundamental responsibilities of a manager and mentor and really not much more:

This includes:

- Advise and counsel in the selection of literary, artistic and musical material.
- Advise and counsel in any and all matters pertaining to publicity, public relations and advertising.
- Advise and counsel with relation to the adoption of proper format for presentation of artist's artistic talents and in the determination of proper style, mood, setting, business and characterization in keeping with Artists talents.
- Advise, counsel and direct in the selection of artistic talent to assist, accompany or embellish artist's artistic presentation.
- Advise and counsel artist with respect to general practices in the entertainment and amusement industries and with respect to such matters of which the artist may have knowledge concerning compensation and privileges extended for similar artistic values.
- Advise and counsel concerning the selection of theatrical agencies and persons, films, and corporations.
- Advise and counsel in any and all matters pertaining to artist's public persona, look and attire.

The final responsibly is to motivate, teach and assist the artist to "STOP MESSING AROUND WITH THEIR LIVES" and "GET THEIR SHINE ON."

As a mentor, I ask, "are you tired of messing around with your life and dreams?" OK, I said it! Then get with the program and make the final commitment to success once and for all. If you have an incredible talent, voice, writing ability, look and marketability then do something about it. Take the time to think about what makes those other successful organizations stick out that seem to easily glide down the river of fame and fortune? Foremost, having talent has a lot to do with the way success grows and leaves behind memorable experiences. Be heard, get noticed and be the star that you are. You must shine brighter than the next competitor. You must take the risk and go out on the ledge to survive. It is amazing what altering your persona, look and attitude can have on your future. You need to shine, shine, shine so you obviously stand out differently than all the other artists and bands. This goes for your music as well. It is required to be different, unconventional and creative. If you want to be taken seriously as an artist or band ask yourself are you ready to be presented to the public, agent or record company. If not, then don't. If you're just playing for fun or don't have aspirations of massive commercial success, then quit reading this book and go out and just have some fun. For those who want more, take into consideration all the components of an artist that is necessary to take the elevator to the top floor. Ask yourself, "when the stage curtains rise up, what will the audience see and experience?" Hopefully something amazing and cool that will fuel the fire of anticipation and excitement. Do you have elements of your stage presentation that makes you look totally professional? If not then design or re-design yourself from the ground up, use projection, lighting, build a great looking stage set. Evaluate yourself, what are you wearing? Some new cool fashion or yesterday worn out jogging outfit? I don't care what most believe, you must look like a star. Do you look like a well-oiled organization? Do you have style and are obviously a class act? Are you able to shine out and be bright and memorable? Are you brandable? Would sponsors want to use you to promote their products? These are essential questions to ask yourself.

Don't miss this step. Invest smartly in your image. If you must spend money, then find the money and do it. Not to mention your music must be a no brainer. You should sound good, always ready to perform and strive to be way over the top.

Have you ever gone to hear a band or artist and to your horror have a sound technician working the sound and lighting board that went deaf and blind ten years ago? No matter how good you think you are this scenario could turn the stomachs of most new audiences. You should make sure this does not happen to you at any point.

No matter how good you look, smell and play it does not make a difference if what is being presented is only spooned out at 20% of the quality expected by your new audiences. Just like the deaf sound man scenario the same effect occurs with a bad look, lack of connection, unprofessionalism, boring set design and disconnected artists. I recently watched a new band that invested into a few new affordable LED computer controlled lighting panels that were placed effectively on stage. They used creativity to build visuals that complemented the band and the lyrics. The band was good but visually they were memorable, looked great and did a good job with their show. Remember, this is the show business! This conscious effort makes an astounding difference and builds the confidence that your efforts are turning you into a different class of entertainer. In most cases, you only get one chance with a new audience to shine brightly in their eyes. Always come out of the box swinging and ready to win. Don't make the mistake by doing anything half way.

Now that's what a good Manager and Mentor sounds like, I gave it to you on a silver plate.

"Remember, this is the show business"

Chapter 9
Connecting With Your Audience 101

What does connecting with your audience mean? Why is this chapter so important? For any artist that is determined to make a career out of the entertainment business they need to take the time to determine who their audience is. Is the artist determined to become an internet star, a live performance sensation, or a commercially focused songwriter and singer? This is very important because this determination does have an effect on the efforts needed to measure success.

It is amazing how an artist can fabricate a marketing plan and through cleaver imagination and creativity can establish a huge loyal following from the basement of their home. Why, because they are clever enough and informed enough to create an environment that motivates their worldwide potential fan base to "log in" and obtain more entertainment value from them. Many artists make a huge mistake by trying to replicate other failed approaches because they lack the planning and creativity to develop something new, exciting and worthy of true entertainment value.

When cartoon artists begins the process of creating an animated movie they know their potential audience, the target age and the subject matter so well that they can create for a purpose the final product. They rely on their understanding of the target demographics and what has proven to work and not work. What makes a performing artist any different? If a new or establish artist wants to create a loyal following they need to visualize and ask where are these people and how can I attract them to establish their support base. Why do rappers dress and move the way they do, why do hard rock bands dress and act the way they do, why do country stars wear cowboy boots and hats? Because that is what works for the demographics that they are reaching out to. Believe me, the fans expect it from you. You have to work with their perception in mind. If you do it right they will imitate and follow you. It is OK to change it up to be recognizable. Sure, some artists deviate from the norm but in general the road is already well defined and should be followed.

Most artists stick to the formula to give them a better chance of connecting with the potential fan base. Actually, a band of hard core metal looking players playing bluegrass would cause that hard core country fan to take a double look to see if they just lost their minds. Nothing is wrong with being creative and different but you better be the best at what you do to overcome the acceptance curve of the fan base.

Most new audiences can be brutal and judgmental because they naturally are comparing the new artist to other established artists or their favorites. If an artist is smart they would prepare for this and work hard to gain respect of the potential fans thus establishing a loyal following. Artists that jump on a stage and power through a set of music in hopes that someone will like them don't realize that this behavior may alone be the beginning of the end. A band must ask what does the audience want? What do they need to do to get the reaction an artist desires?

You can pile up a ton of wood boards and stones in front of a house builder and say build a house. You just might be surprised what you might get if the builder is very skilled, organized, knowledgeable, motivated, creative and follows the rules. You can also get a disaster if these same attributes of the builder are not present. The other approach is to know what you are building before you gather the materials and components. The building can be designed for its intended final purpose. Successful performing organizations are built the same way. Broadway musicals, movies, television shows, books, scripts, etc. Bands and artist should follow the same process. If you are a rap group don't expect to please everyone in the blue grass world or the electronica arena.

First learn your demographics. Where are the people that are most impressionable? The music business is just like any other business. Money exchanges hands for specific products in each industry. In the music business, the money is exchanged by the consumer for concert tickets, artist merchandise, music media (CD, Downloads) that's it. So, focus on these products. That is where the money is. What does your demographic spend their money on?

Like it or not, money drives and fuels sustained success and puts fuel in the tour bus. Therefore, all bands and artist should gear and focus their marketing efforts in those specific areas of commerce. This being addressed, why would someone want to buy a t-shirt, a CD or come to a concert. Think about it. There is a reason and a smart band or artist must create that reason. It begins with knowing your audience. You should create real memories and so they feel they took something home that is part of you. Stop for just one minute and stand on the edge of the stage and acknowledge your audience's existence. Who are these people? Take a moment before you play or sing a note and try to smile at and look at every one of them. You must first try to connect with them if they are going to give you a chance to connect with you. You don't even have to say a word really. You have to invite them into your life as well. You have a responsibility to them. As soon as you stop assuming the responsibly of connecting with your audience the slide into oblivion will begin. If you can do this and think this way 90% of the struggle will come to an end. You should go out of your way to appreciate them in ways no other would. You must be approachable. Your talent and creative art just completes the picture, it is a tool.

Why do artists sit on the edge of the stage or slap hands, throw picks and drum sticks and sometimes their clothes. This is a simple way of connecting. I ask what is wrong with giving a signed picture or a card with a free upload to every person who comes to your concert? Why not come out after your set and make a point to thank everyone you can and ask their name. Perhaps get your picture taken with everyone in the club and post it on social media. Most bands get on stage, ram through their set then exit the back door and hang out in a back room for the rest of the night. Your audience will embrace you if you embrace them. You should master the skill of managing your own behavior when it comes to meeting and making friends. That also goes with meeting and introducing yourself to everyone who can help you in your journey and connect with them. Being to cool for school will not get you anywhere. This business of "Becoming the Idol" takes serious effort and work.

Why do you think it is such a cool thing to be given VIP status at a hotel, club or concert? This is because its makes you feel appreciated and special. You make someone feel special and appreciated from your heart, especially audiences and it will pay dividends.

This reminds me of a special story that still to this day I cannot forget. My wife and I were producing a large outdoor concert in Portland. There were three hugely popular bands playing for a major radio station promotion. Typical concert scene with bouncers guarding the backstage fence door. Thousands of fans everywhere. Knowing everyone and being the producer, I moved around to different areas of the concert arena. My wife and I had back stage passes hanging from our necks when we noticed these two young ladies trying with all their might to see through the cracks of the fence. They had their autograph books, band t-shirts and hats on, the works. At the same time my wife and I looked at each other and said "yes" let's do it. We walk up to the gate where my bouncers were and leaned out and kindly asked the two young ladies to step inside the gate. They pointed at each other and said, "Who us?" They made their way through the crowd and entered the gate. My wife and I took our back stage passes off and said we want you to have these. We asked them to blend in and be respectful and have the time of your lives. The expressions, tears and shock on their faces were priceless as we led them back to the service tents and let them in. In those tents were their idols. Why not right? A bit of time went by and my wife and I walked into the food services buffet tent and in line to get food were these two brightly smiling friends standing in line talking with all their idols. It actually made our day. The point is folks you can make the day for others from the stage if you try. You are in control of the situation. Audiences are exactly the same. These people came to see you. They went out of there way and spent their money to see you. They travel distances to see you. Don't make the mistake and miss the opportunity to connect. Never disappoint your following or your audience family.

"This business of Becoming the Idol takes serious effort and work"

Chapter 10
Where is My Record Deal?

Another major "Dream Stealer" resides with the misconception that if the artist can spend countless hours recording flawless recordings, clever bridges, one of a kind guitar sounds, cool lyrical hooks and apply unbelievable mastering techniques they will surely be accepted and adored by all. Furthermore, the expectation that all the major records companies will surly do the same and become mysteriously transfixed and send multi-Million-dollar recording, marketing, publishing and distribution contracts is far from the truth. Someone forgot to tell all the home studio musical geniuses that there are millions of other cleaver people expecting exactly the same results.

With the current invent and ease of acquiring high quality home recording equipment that is now available to just about anyone, the flood of home based music production is nothing less than a tsunami of substandard material. This material in most cases is not backed up by live performance or anything else that resembles true entertainment value. Most star struck artists spend every dollar of their rent money, car payments, credit card payments, medical insurance money and live on minimal budgets to create their recordings. They do this with great hopes that someone will call and offer them the deal of a life time. Therefore, 99% of these creators send out their recording to the record companies, cast out their EPKs to the wind, join every internet collective in hope that someone will notice them and love them. Unfortunately, getting lost in the song tsunami sends a message that no one wants to experience.

This actual process is nothing but a huge "Dream Stealer" to the majority of the artists entering the revolving door of dreams and despair. Perhaps the problem is that the focus is on the wrong objective in the first place although the intent was humble, respectful and admirable. In these cases, many artists believe this result was due to the fact that the music was not good enough, timing was wrong or needs to be more unique. Therefore, the majority set off on repeating the same process all over again and not even giving the previous completed works the glimmer of a chance. Created and produced music are like scripts to TV and movies. They are the basis and building blocks for some other completed interpretation that establishes or builds commercial entertainment value. This is even true for the band or artist who created it. The music is the foundation, not all that is created is worthy of commercial investment no matter how much an artist is connected to the finished product.

Even as a seasoned entertainment management professional it continues to amaze me how unknown, new, unproven struggling artists don't listen to advice, or educate themselves on the realities of their chosen profession. I am approached daily from all over the world by artists seeking my services as professional Manager. I receive countless emails, phone calls and referrals on a regular basis. I find it exciting and rewarding that my name and credibility have given me a place in the mechanics of this business. However, I started to realize many common traits and behaviors of artists that to this day remain a constant with little variation.

Here is an example of the basic contact I get from most of the artists seeking help or trying to find a professional Manager:

"Dear Mr. Jaworski, please excuse me in advance for intruding, I know you are a busy person but I wanted to introduce myself to you. My name is S. Jackson, I am an artist and am looking for professional management to take my music to the next level. I would appreciate if you could review my attached EPK and links to all of my web based media sites, videos, pictures, bios, reviews, magazine clippings, testimonial and lyrical library. I am passionate about my music and I am getting well known in my area. I would like to talk to you about my goals and plans. Peace, S. Jackson."

To be perfectly frank with you, I enjoy and appreciate these requests. In the grand scheme of things to be given respect for my position inspires me. I always review everything that is given to me. This is out of the gold prospector DNA in me. In fact, my hobby is prospecting in the gold bearing hills of Colorado. Believe me, I know how much rock that must be moved before you find that shinny nugget. We will talk later about the similarities that exists between prospecting for gold in the hills and prospecting for gold records in the music market.

After responding and talking with thousands of inspired and budding artists whose dreams and desires are excreted from every pore of their bodies, I found a way to narrow down the key elements that allows the true characteristics of high potential to emerge. I am hopeful you will understand this very important point as to why I have proceeded only with the best deserving artists.

Instead of going into all of the typical embellishments, praises, and allowing an artist to tell me how fantastic and amazing they are, I ask three specific questions. The following questions are a result of countless years of experience, successes, disappointments and wastes of time and money.

I always confront the inquiring artist with the same three questions and I do expect an honest response from them:

Question 1: Where are you in your career that you believe you need a professional manager?

Question 2: Are you in the music business or the entertainment business?

Question 3: If you had a professional manager what would you expect of that person?

I am sure, to your surprise, only about 5 percent of all inquiries respond back. I contribute this behavior as an example and result of the overall statistics of the number of people who are successful in generating a successful career in any given profession. I don't want to mention the dilemma of appeasing bruised ego's that feel insulted for questioning their level of achievement. That is another side effect of dealing with temperamental artists. However, the majority of the people who do respond are mixed with defiance or pure honestly. I think you will find these responses enlighten and interesting. Some of the answers are as little as two words and as long as a college dissertation. Either way, I appreciate the feedback.

Typical response to the questions:

Question #1: Where are you in your career that you believe you need a professional manager? The usual answer three out of five times is: "It is the established managers that have all the contacts that will help me get to the next level" or "It is only the managers that are allowed access to the people I need to lift me up." The answers to this question are WRONG.

Question 2: Are you in the music business or the entertainment business? Again, the top answer three out of five times is: "the music business." This answer is again WRONG. Everyone forgets this is the entertainment business.

Question 3: If you had a professional manager what would you expect of this person? The top answer given four out of five times is: I would expect my manager to find me a big record deal and book me gigs. Again, WRONG. Remember, this topic is very important to those who are trying to do the right things for their career.

Missing the point to these questions indicates a lack of understanding of the natural processes leading to difficulties that will emerge in the future.

The right answer to Question Number One:
This is a test of the artist's common sense. A manager is a mentor, a coach, a challenger and an asset of untold value that is focused on guiding the artist to their own success. They are not salesmen. Not understanding the rules of the road in regards to others accepting the responsibility to work and invest their time on the artist's behalf is unacceptable. This could become problematic for an artist to move forward in their career. The artist must be the commander of their own existence. Everyone has heard this statement countless times that "nothing is impossible." I beg to differ, but with the right dedicated help from others, focused intent, keen preparation,

utilizing expert knowledge and experience, accepting directed and devoted trust anything is possible.

Try climbing to the top of Mt. Everest all by yourself or trying to land on the moon all by yourself, this is surely impossible. The fact is, achieving success in the entertainment business is very much the same. However, many don't believe that it is possible to become successful all by themselves by creating their future one fan at a time. It depends on the speed at which success is to be expected though one's own efforts in this business and not the responsibility of someone else. Let us move on.

The right answer to Question Number Two:

All artists have to understand they are in the "Business of Entertainment" not the selling of music business. If an artist is capable of successfully entertaining any given audience, then the sale of material goods becomes the responsibility of the music business machine. People only pay for something that excites them, something that satisfies a need or want or something that entertains them. An artist needs to stop for moment and understand the power comes from delivering entertainment value in bags full. This is the job of the Idol. Entertaining your way to success day after day, week after week, tour after tour.

The magical thing about building quality entertainment is that you don't have to be the best musician or performers in the world.

The catcher is you must be memorable in the execution of your entertainment plan and deliver the goods flawlessly. After that the rest goes on autopilot. This is what most music executives want to hear and see from budding superstars. This is the business of entertainment! Finally,

The right answer to Question Number Three:
The manager is not responsible for landing a record deal. It is the hard work and dedication of the artist that must create a commercially viable business opportunity that attracts the power companies. The manager is an essential coach that should be instrumental in guiding the process but it is the artist that must put the glitter on it. You will know when you have achieved that level because the people who will make a difference in your future will tell you so. They will let you know when they see potential in you. The manager can help that process but you the artist are responsible 100% of the time to prepare for that moment.

"Dream Stealer" # 1245: Don't think for one minute that just because of some manager's name dropping or claims of access to powerful influences that they can get you a deal. It is only your attention to excellence in entertainment presentation that flips the switch on your career. You alone are responsible for your future.

Chapter 11

So, You Want To Become A Star

In my process of evaluating artists for the possibility of investing my time and resources I find it very important to interview an artist extensively to draw out very critical information. This process is a necessary function not only to provide me with the information I need but to minimize my risk. Therefore, I must again have answers to specific questions:

1) Does this artist or band really have what it takes to make it?
2) Do they understand what they are doing?
3) Do they understand if they are responsible enough to deserve the big players working on their behalf?

Most people in my position truly want to help guide and create the next Idol or help fire up a successful career of a deserving artist or band. These questions are equivalent to asking a group of ambitious fifteen-year-old amateur explorers, "So you want to go to the Great Ice Cliffs of the Frozen Zimanian Artic Zone?" Do you know what that involves and the huge commitment you will be agreeing to? Do you understand the bottom line reality?

Let's take this following scenario into the light. Let's take the example of a very talented five-piece band who believe they are ready to go. They are well-rehearsed, they have a completed CD and in their minds they are ready for the big time. In this scenario, they have asked me to manage them. Being a realist please pay attention to the following reality check. I usually skip right to the final act and present the seriousness of the decisions they are contemplating.

In this light, I would start with: "So let me get this straight, you want to live on a bus for the next 6 months? OK, I would like to ask each of you something important. Do any of you have car payments, medical payments, credit card payments, apartment rent or mortgage payments, insurance payments, child support payments, musical equipment payments or have bill collectors after you? Exactly how much money will each of you need monthly to support your financial obligations or perhaps a family? What would happen if you were to quit your job and tour extensively? The reason for these questions is to strike up the reality of the responsibility and requirements of their decision to pursue a future in the entertainment business. Believe me, only a few can survive the questioning here before the blank faces appear.

The reality check here is, even if all of the members only needed a minimum of $40K per year (which is not that much these days) just to pay their bills while they were on tour. A total of $200,000 net income would need to be generated just to pay the basic bills back home. This does not include a sound man who doubles as a roadie and tech, so let us add another $40,000 because this person has bills as well. There will be miscellaneous expenses added to the total. At a minimum let's add an additional $15,000. Most likely at the beginning the band will have very basic transportation expenses (perhaps a van). At the beginning promoters are not going to pay a new band high end transportation expenses or classy hotels rooms. No matter what, there will be unforeseen expenses so let us use a conservative $10,000.00 for the additional "Out of Pocket Costs." Add all of this together and that is now $ 265,000.00 needed just to put this band on the road for one-year. This is the basic bottom line with no unseen nightmares (which there will be). Let's add another 10 % for that. The total is now $291500.00. This is the amount needed just to pay the basic band members bills. Once I go through this reality check the room starts to get quiet. So I ask again, "are you are willing to go on the road full time, build your fan base, live in cheap hotels, eat crappy food and send all your money back home to pay your bills and have no money in your pockets? If the answer is yes then here comes the clincher. This means bottom line, than you will have to play at least 100 gigs for $3000.00 each just to pay the bills back home. Oh, let's not forget the 10% Manager fees and the 10% Booking Agent fees (if you can find a reputable ones willing to actually do the job). Let's add another $600.00 to each gig. The magic number is now $3600.00 per gig just to break even The final question I ask is, has your band ever played one gig for $3600.00?

Actually, I have never met a promoter or club owner who will pay that kind of money for a totally unknown original band or artist. At this point I usually get a blank stare and the rebound response is "That is why we need a label to give us the tour support we need." Most believe their success and support is expected to be someone else's risk. The artist must know they have a shot based on their efforts to create something that is worth someone else's risk. That is why I intervene and insist that this is why you must align properly and make yourself into a bonified investment opportunity before you try to climb Mt Everest. You must be worth the risk.

A serous artist must gain and develop the skills, knowledge, recognition and other attributes that will allow the opportunity to take the next step.

Step number one is always "Development of and proof of Entertainment Value." You are not worth anything to an investor, label or corporation until you can prove your worth. Are you in or out? This is where most of my preliminary vetting conversations terminate and traditionally I rarely hear from the band again. You would think I asked them to commit to climbing Mt. Everest next week or give all their blood or something like that. The reality is most are looking for the easy way or are simply delusional.

The truth is, this is one of the most difficult businesses in the universe and it should be clearly understood before attempting to ascend to the summit. At this point I become the "Dream Stealer."

Not really, just the person who has the respect of the artist to show the path and not paint such a picture of false impressions that someone is so good that they base all their decisions on artificial perceptions.

In every city worldwide there are thousands of rehearsal rooms occupied by the "next best thing." The truth be told, some are certainly destined for huge careers. I have personally met many of them that went on to stellar careers. They all had something in common. That is, they created something of true commercial value that they designed from the start. They took serous efforts to make themselves valuable.

The discovery process for the corporate beneficiaries of the commercial end user is in place and functions quite nicely. The system has not changed much over the years but for some reason the established system of success is constantly trying to be bypassed in cleaver and useless ways. If you were a gold prospector and only because you were persistent, stuck with the process, learned about what you were looking for, and proceeded in a sensible and deliberate manner your chances of discovering and uncovering a fabulous deposit of gold is quite good. The problem is this valuable deposit is 25 miles out in the middle of the desert with no roads and you only can carry minimal equipment, water and food. How would you be able to make a commercial success out of it? The fact is you have the gold deposit. Where are you going to get the massive resources, financial backing and manpower to dig it up to make a commercial success of it. The same goes for talented bands and artists. The gold is there it just needs to be resourced, developed and properly managed to cash in. Major record companies are very happy to take over your claim and pay you a small royalty perhaps ten to fifteen percent of the net proceeds. These minimum royalties will most likely pay for all the costs of developing the road to the mine and most of the startup costs. For some reason, most creative artist believe that the gold is going to magically fly out of the ground all by itself.

There is always a massive financial risk for someone. To become a Star there is a price to pay. If you can do it under your own ambition, enthusiasm and sacrifice then great. But if an artist and band applies the proven systems currently in place the outcome and rewards could be much more in line with the long-term career goals they are seeking.

This is a chess game you play with yourself and with the entire industry. You have to be willing to create winning opportunities for others to gain from your dedicated efforts. Your art is the vehicle you just need a dedicated and supportive crew to win the race. Don't let the "Me, Me, Me" infection make you undesirable. Become the investment everyone wants. This will bring you closer to your goal than anything else. If done right getting paid $3,600.00

a show could be the beginning and peanuts to your true earning potential.

There is an area of concern that I have come across time after time with original and collaborating artistic minds and that is the "Don't worry bro, it's all cool with everything we do together, we will share equally in everything." When seeking a major investment deal, the players have to be realistic of how the money gets spilt up and give credit where credit is due. This concept is all peaches and cream at the beginning of most professional collaborative relationships. But as time progresses the gray areas and fundamental flaws of this type of relationship start to emerge. Like any marriage of the mind or traditional marriage most of the difficult situations that destroy relationships don't emerge until time passes. This fundamental reality is sure to touch most emerging artists at one point or another. There is a defined cycle of creation and destruction that occurs within most musical organizations. It is a fact that these entities will last only a certain time and duration until they either become creatively stagnant or internal relationships and different professional perspectives injects its poison into the mix.

If one looks around they will note that only a very small handful of established bands or artists seem to remain together and "Live the Life" they originally worked so hard to obtain. One of the main reasons is, "that is just the way it is." Life's trials, economics, age, time, mis-guided intentions, and lack of knowledge all lead up to the ultimate demise of most musical organizations. The cycle all start with a moment of inspiration, the meeting of creative minds, innocent desires, and perhaps a jam session or single public performance. Using the example of the jam session, musicians have a knack of getting together for a bit of fun and release of creative energy. The fact that magically a "New" sound is somehow created, musical tastes collide and talents merge that expand new ideas into a fresh new life. From the simple act of playing a few songs together sets the stage for yet another jam session and emerging new opportunity with a new chance to continue the journey.

The making of bands is very much like a new personal relationship. They start off fresh and new, full of excitement, bright visions, galactic dreaming, carefree attitudes and tight ever binding relationships. They take the path of least resistance and emerge as a combination of all parts and the pieces bound together for the common goal of the enjoyment of the musical experience. As time flow forward the organizing starts to take shape with a more defined existence, purpose and direction. For some this is good if the direction is based on common sense, focused intent and meaningful purpose to exist. For the majority this becomes the fuse to self-destruction, broken dreams, differences in opinion, resentment and regrets. Sad as it may be, the journey is littered with the results of the repeated mistakes that kill most budding careers and goals of achieving the huge record deal.

There is one reality that most striving artists must take to heart. The big deal is just not going to drop in their laps. The fact is the major record companies are like any other business. They exist to make a profit. In most cases, they base all their decisions to invest into an artist because they know they will make a return on their investment. The average majority of artists look at these companies as the only limiting step between stardom, acceptability, and complete success. Bring signed is the goal of achieving Nirvana. The industry sets the stakes and the trends. Technology has recently changed the stakes, but in the process created opportunity from the rubble of a once dynamic industry. The independent artist today is an entrepreneur first and must do whatever they can to stop the normal cycle of destruction and re-creation.

"Live the life that you worked so hard to obtain"

Chapter 12
Success by Design

Rarely does one stop to think that the successful movie or band they just watched and loved was designed from the bottom up to have the structure and framework to be successful in the commercial market place. Most consumers of commercial music could care less about the technical efforts and production efforts needed to complete the finished product. All they care about is if they got their monies worth of thrills, visuals and audio stimulation that they expect.

One cannot imagine the tens of thousands of feet of film lying on the floor of the editing room or the countless tracks erased trying to find that perfect sound or performance. The focused attention on the affect and expectation of the project alone will dictate the outcome. The life of the artist and the project depends on it.

What makes musical artists any different in today's world? Most artists don't understand the concept of how a career is built on the quality of the last performance. Leaving the audience wanting more is the goal. This goes for not just the finished commercial product but the live performance as well. The live performance is the human connection needed to sustain any future growth of the artist or artistic venture. How many times have you personally gone to a concert of your favorite recording artist only leaving feeling let down and disappointed never to buy another recording from them? You ask yourself was I satisfied? If you were not, then a little bit of the air comes out of the balloon.

A successful artistic venture starts with vision and true talent development. During the onset of those sparks of brilliance that each artist experiences a few times in their life something unique happens and when it does this magic must be built on. If acted upon with the right design, then there can be an opportunity to take the risk. To take the risk you should make sure you are willing to take it all the way to the top.

Ask yourself what are you designing? Writing songs is just one part of the effort. A new sound, look, fad or beat? The term used in the music business is "Original Artist." simply said the artist is "One of a Kind" and unique to anything else. Why would the masses be drawn to something that is "One of a Kind?" The only logical answer to this is the artist must be so memorable that they are never forgotten for some spectacular thing that they do. Something that is so special and memorable that it becomes timeless and branded to them thus becoming "One of A Kind" and a bonified "Original Artist." It should be designed that way from the beginning.

You can do exactly this if you take the time to use your talent and vision in unconventional ways. If you don't have this vision, there are many people out there that do and you need to actively seek them out and work it out together. You may be exquisitely talented as players or a band but don't pass go in the live performance section or able to create something meaningful at the entertainment design chalkboard. Think about each popular artist that you like. What did they do that hooked you? What are they doing that is so unique that turned you around to their existence? Really think about this. You must take the time to pay attention. Your chances of making it in this business depends on it. Success is by design not an accident. Upon each waking moment, you should be focused on working out the details. The next step is to create it and then follow through. Go on your journey and enjoy every minute of it because that is what will give you the courage to do it again and again. You will be surprised at what you can create of commercial value if you design it that way and have a purpose to create it. What is your purpose in life? I guess to become a popular musical artist with a life-long career as an entertainer or you would not be reading this book.

Chapter 13
Don't Be a Bridge Burner

If there is one element that is more damaging and destructive to a future career in this business than any other, that would be burning your valuable bridges. This "Dream Stealer" is right up at the top of the list.

When an artist becomes an active member of the entertainment industry they will cross paths with countless movers and shakers of the industry. Some of these people are destined to take the place of their peers and predecessors in high and powerful places. The bottom line is you never know who is going to "make it" to those prized and influential positions. These influential positions can be executives of major music and entertainment media companies, Managers, Producers, Creative Directors, Agents, Music Directors, Program Director and countless others that are influential in driving a successful career.

Most artists, yes, I'm talking about you, have a problem with constructive criticism. Constructive criticism fans the fiery state of resentment. It is the catalyst for creating separation between creative people and business professionals. This separation burns holes in the bridges of success. Resentment in the hands of the person who allows such a destructive emotion to enter their life can create the poison of rejection. With this poison, most will find themselves being rejected from the circles that they need so desperately. It creates a foul taste in everyone's mouth and there is no cure. It is a small world within the commercial music industry and there are a few big players that count.

Next, close mindedness shuts all the door of opportunity for those who seek entrance into a very defined and finite world. It always baffles me when I am pursued and asked to review a bands performance or their recordings and no one wants to hear my true assessment if it is not full of praise. To give respect and fulfill my obligations as a professional, I do it. When I am provided the question "so what do you think?" I prepare myself for the "you are full of garbage" rebuttal. Ninety-five percent of the time it turns out quite badly because no one wants to hear the truth. The suggestions offered may not even relate to performance or music quality. In fact, it may be a simple suggestion about image, market share or a simple constructive observation.

A band or artist can have the hottest sound and the killer players but they may lack marketability because they are just a complete and total bore. I have no problem offering extreme complements and show how speechless I am about great works. However, I am not afraid of expressing my distaste in worthless stage presentation or run of the mill attitude towards not creating sound entertainment content.

Let's face it, learning the concept of turning audiences into fans is like poking a gorilla in the eye to most striving artists. The first thing any artist should know is what they are trying to accomplish with their art before they ask the big question "Did you like it?" My response is usually, "are you happy with your own performance?" Nevertheless, we are talking about burning bridges. Just because someone does not get the same jolt as you do from your creation does not mean they deserve a negative response from you. A humble artist is special and different then the self-centered ego maniac that gets every door slammed behind them. This music business is a business of appreciation of someone else's skills and meaningful consideration. This goes for the working of the musical unit itself not just the outside industry contacts.

There must be complete respect for each one of the contributing members of the family. You someday may need them and most likely will. It is imperative that everyone you meet is given respect and consideration because if you don't the family unit will fall apart and so will your dreams.

You make it to the top of this business by taking all the deserving contributors to the mountain with you. In retrospect, when most music executives encounters a disrespectful, and self-centered talent they become extremely careful when deciding if it is worth the trouble to get on the bus with them. Yes, I have seen this for myself. Just because an artist was difficult and demanding and disrespectful they passed on investing into their future. Thus, the bridge gets burnt to a crisp. Along with the situation created by this behavior, a side effect usually sucks every other close relationship into the black hole with it. Never forget that others are and can be investing their time and money into you.

If you take out a loan from anyone, you have an obligation to satisfy the loan based on your agreement. This loan can be of something other than money. It can be any kind of help given to you, references given to you, creative input offered from other talents individuals, creative support, gratis services or investment of professional support and lastly don't forget about taking care of your fans. If these faithful gestures are not taken into consideration as your career develops expect the smell of burning bridges to start permeating the room. You cannot afford to alienate one single person. The final step in preventing a catastrophic failure is always maintaining your cool as if losing one relationship is unacceptable. Being humble, approachable, likable, respectable, positive, workable and flexible will extinguish most of the embers that are just waiting to flare up and incinerate your future. It does not take much to become an undesirable in this business. An unprofessional attitude or taking advantage of someone's kind nature or knowledge that has supported you during the difficult times will get you burned.

If this behavior persists then it is only a matter of time before you lose your edge and drift away and out of sight.

"Remember Always, this is the entertainment business"

Chapter 14
You Can Imitate Yourself Right into Oblivion

For all those artists that want to follow the path most traveled and still believe that the "Big Record Deal" is the goal then you may gain from a bit of wisdom offered in this chapter.

Times have changed in regards to how cleaver new artists are reinventing the way the music industry rotates. However, there still are ruminates of some very powerful entities that continue to operate following the traditional ways of a different and robust commercial industry. The industry has simply changed into a different process with different players. This includes commercial entities that have nothing to do with the music business itself. They are entrepreneurs and investors with limitless marketing and business management resources.

If a band or artist does not have the knowledge, drive, ambition and know how to promote themselves to stardom then there still are those that have the resources and power to move an artist along. If this is the path, then put yourself in their place. Ask yourself would you invests massive dollars into your future? How about a million dollars? If you choose to take the self-promotion and marketing route how much time and money would you be willing to invest or lose? When would you expect a return on your investment? If you are going to make a difference in your future, you cannot have an open-ended deal for a return on your time and investment. How can you expect the outside investor not to require the same? You must provide the assurances that you will be able to breakout running. The bottom line is, if your musical endeavors have the right stuff then the natural process will bring you to cross the paths of some unique people who recognize commercial opportunities.

Attracting the power players to take the hook is your full-time job. The investor must have a product that can win and open new opportunities. They do not want to depend on cheap imitations or cleaver knock-offs. Certainly, unique trends can spin off similar successful organizations that are able to take a short ride on the popularity train but the real power comes from being an identifiable singularity from the beginning.

The first thing a major investor or commercial entity will do is to evaluate a new and promising artist or entertainer on how unique they are. Is the product cutting edge and timely? Second, how identifiable is the act and is it brandable? Third, is the artist approachable, real, memorable and have natural charisma. Finally, there must be a substantial history of a natural following being generated behind the scenes. The bottom line is, does your organization have the potential to generate a substantial revenue out of the gate for the act itself and the investor?

Remember, investors have the luxury of the pick of the litter, the best of the best. They know the risks. The last thing an investment group wants is an act or product that appears artificial, grossly fabricated or nothing but a copycat. They have the clear choice to make and the power to provide the right artist or band with the financial support needed to ride the wave.

Investors come in many forms, family, friends, businesses, sponsors and major music industry players. What each has in common is they don't want to lose their money. What motivates an investor? What are they looking for? Certainly, a business opportunity that is fresh and new. Now that we have clearly defined the path you must consider this very important perception of the business you are participating in, it must be fool proof.

The entire music industry is like a rainbow with many different colors. Each color represents a different type or style of music. For example, country music can be represented by Blue, Rock-Red and Rap-Green. Each are very different but unique to their particular market (Color). To break this down a bit further and to make a point, let's consider this analogy. Within the blue segment of the music business rainbow there may be various and different shades of blue. For example, if we look at the country market represented by blue, light blue can represent- bluegrass country, dark blue -

country rock, aqua blue - classic country and baby blue - urban country. Each shade can have its own following and specific audience. The red color could easily represent rock, green - electronica, purple – jazz, yellow – heavy metal. There are countless possibilities and shades that can represent individual markets and each shade has its own stars.

Successful and popular new stars and idols are created in each market every year that are completely disassociated from one another. Remember there a billions of people on the earth that in majority like music, entertainment and live performance. Each of these people are mostly likely to fall into one of the shades of the music rainbow. Your color is your audience and you must become identifiable to your audience in one way or another. It is just fine not to be liked by everyone in all the color sets.

All artists and musical groups have their influences that define their direction but this can be unhealthy if imitation becomes the primary formula for success. It is the natural affinity to migrate to a style or shade of music but imitation is only acceptable if one learns from the success elements of the past. In this case the artist must deliberately extract the positive effects and apply them for a new approach or creative efforts. That is a mouthful but this is the facts. As an example, an artist or band can extract and update a much older successful musical works and with their own creative efforts modify the basics just enough to make it current again. This can be done with any style and shade of the rainbow.

Trying to ride the success of another successful artist's efforts does not create the uniqueness that the major investors are looking for. But success by design can change the direction of any artist if this basic principle can be utilized to its fullest. Creative artists are the reason for the evolution of new styles, trends and breakthroughs in this industry so start thinking that way. Don't try to imitate yourself into a rut.

A good career can be built covering a style or tapping into an existing audience but at any given time only one or two can fill the top spot. We are talking about "Becoming the Idol" here. You must become a one of a kind, pick a color and stick with it and evolve into something new. Don't be a copycat, be a shapeshifter, become a blend of a new tastes and the beginning of a new era. That is where the massive support you will need will come from.

"Don't be a Copycat, be a Shapeshifter"

Chapter 15
Finding Your Middle C, Tuning In

As a little boy, I have always have been fascinated with music. I am sure this comes from my childhood being exposed to music by my father. In my father's time, he became one of the best musicians in the business. He was one of the top professional musicians of the big band swing era. All the big names at that time wanted him to join them on the road. He was a true musician, music was in his DNA. He was the real deal.

He started playing professionally at the age of 14 and was on the road. Destined to become a star, he was fortunate to make a great living his entire life with music. This is what most budding stars strive to achieve. Even late in his life he still had the magic touch. I learned a life time worth of knowledge about the music business from him. Now it is my time to share it with you.

I would sit for hours and ask him to play for me and tell me stories about his journeys throughout the music and entertainment business. I must tell you, the time I spent with him was priceless. If he had not shared his early life and told me about his amazing journey in the early music industry I would not have this opportunity to share it with you through this book. I experienced firsthand what it was like to become and live as a name musician. I have grown to appreciate all artist who strive for the same opportunities to do what they feel they are born to do in life. Watching many of my friends and artists that I have worked with actually breakthrough the barrier I am now confident to draw reasonable conclusions to the common threads that define the true nature of the entertainer and the music business.

My earliest memories of my father coming home after being on the road for months still sticks in my mind. It would begin with the thud of his instrument cases on the kitchen floor. I was quick to search his tattered brown cases for new stickers that had accumulated from all over the world. Then the smiles and hugs and a rare instance of a sit-down family dinner. He would tell stories of all the places he has been. He would be home for a few weeks and then gone again. I still remember while he was away my mother would put all the kids in front of the TV and we would see our father playing with the top TV stars and other music legends. I was always very proud of that and always fascinated. The under draft of this imaginary perception of a fairytale life was bound with countless months of separation and short lived family togetherness. This is truly the scourge of the entertainment business…family separation. But I knew someday I wanted to experience the same. I now must share with you the things that opened my life to the music business. It all started with that one note.

I must have been 3 of 4 years old, I remember my father coming home and one evening sitting with him near the fireplace. He hung a huge saxophone around my neck. It might as well have been a tuba. I remember he also had a sax in his hand. He put the instrument to my mouth and said "now put this mouth piece in your mouth like this and blow very steady and hard." To my surprise, out of nowhere blasted a solid nicely toned note. I remember the look on my father's face of amazement. He said "holy cow that sounded great." I was so happy. He immediately showed me how to put my little fingers on the holes on the horn and within a few minutes had me playing a little song. He said "well kid, I guess you did not fall to far from the tree." He picked up his horn and played with me. I remember my mother taking a photo of the moment that I still have today. Little did I know this was going to become the beginning of my entire entertainment business career. One simple gesture changed my life. That is why I am hopeful the simple gesture of this book will also inspire the next generation of managers, producers, artists, performers and entertainers.

Soon thereafter, my father purchased a piano. I was perhaps about 4 or 5 years old. One day he sat me at the piano and he took my finger and placed it on the middle C key and pushed it down and said "this is the C in the middle and this is note number 1." He then immediately pointed to the note on the sheet music and said "this is note number 1, the C in the middle and remember that." He then asked me to turn my back and he said "now listen," as he hit the same note and said "this is the C in the middle note number 1." He played that same note repeatedly with my back turned. Little did I know that this is the note that calibrated my music mind and creativity forever.

Over the months to come, he repeated this process until we visited every key on the piano and showed me each note on the sheet music. This happened before I was even taught to play any songs. He was teaching me the basics, the foundation, the beginning to it all, one note at a time without me knowing it. But most importantly, he was tuning my ear.

He made it fun, memorable, and rewarding. Next appeared a teacher who connected the notes to the music. Within two years I was playing anything put in front of me first pass. In no time, I was playing as a special guest in front of orchestras and live stage performances. My key life changing experience was at eight years old when I played a 15-minute solo of difficult classics selections to a packed performing arts theater. When I was playing, I remember it was dead silent except for my piano, I could barely reach the pedals. I remember sitting on the edge of the seat looking at my fingers, at the C in the middle and then looked up at my father in the front of the audience with tears in his eyes. Then I heard the people, standing and applauding and cheering it seemed like forever. I have never experienced anything like that again during my entire career playing in bands and other musical experiences. In a childish humbleness, this never went to my head but I never forgot about it either. I know what desire of the stage is. I know why so many people work so hard for the opportunity and I know the drive and heart of a creative person and what is inside.

I learned the business the hard way. I had my music, my dreams, daydreams and imagination that allowed me to journey into the creative world of the entertainment business. I would not have it any other way.

My father spent many hours with me answering many of my questions about his experience in the music business, life on the road, the problems, heartaches, pitfalls and rewards. I also learned plenty before I exercised my own liberties in the business and developed a keen sense of why certain music and entertainment works and others do not. I learned the magic of taking and learning from the infinite wisdom of someone who had taken the journey for real.

My life transitioned into finding other amazing talented and incredible people with the same dreams and aspirations. I have taken a broad look at the music industry as a whole. As complicated as it may seem it is quite simple once you look past all the smoke and mirrors. It is about basic human desire, needs and normal behavior. I feel confident I have identified the traits, behaviors, outside influences, processes and other realities that prevent these amazing people from achieving their ultimate levels of success. The number one attribute to success is being calibrated and tuning into the processes required to make it happen. I call that "Finding your Middle C." All artists must find a way to remain grounded and take it back to the innocence of the process to keep it alive.

Achieving the level of success you desire does not happen by accident. Success is a result of a focused well defined process. Everything on earth is a result of some type of process. Think about it. Just being born, making a sandwich, producing a stage show, driving a car from point A to B or simply weaving a blanket. Without the defined process there cannot be success, no products and no achievement. What makes an artist any different? A growth and development process also must be applied. I am always impressed when I see a performer or artist following a defined process to achieve the expected impact value. Impact is what an audience desires and expects to allow you inside their memories, their book of favorite "must see artists," thus creating a fan. The fan is the most valuable asset to an artist. The fan's loyalty is only earned based upon the impact and value they themselves are willing to accept.

The ultimate goal of any performing artist is to turn audiences into fans. An audience can be one person or thousands. But the fact is fans are earned one performance at a time. We all have had an experience of going to a concert and although in a fantastic concert venue to only then be disappointed by a bad or boring performance. In addition, we were completely baffled as to why a favorite band or performing act was not what we expected. In these cases, the artist generally has lost touch with the process that works and is no longer tuned into the fan's expectations. The same goes for opening acts for some of the major artists we paid good money to see. I ask you, can you remember the name of the last opening band you watched. Why not? That cannot happen to you, PERIOD. Find your Middle C and calibrate yourself to perform at your best.

"Impact is what an audience desires and expects from you"

Chapter 16
Prospecting for Gold Records

The only way you will find gold is to know where to find it, know how it is created and learn what tools you need and how to dig it out? It is a process. Gold is where you find it. Many artists should study the success stories of the prospectors that forged up the mountains to the gold fields. The process remains the same, simple changes do occur in regards to implementation of new technologies and tools but the fundamentals stays the same. When you decide you want to prospect for gold and platinum records you will find that there are "Dream Stealers" everywhere. Because this process is something very few understand and the "know it all's and naysayers" are quick to offer great advice such as "Don't waste your time, you don't have enough money to be in that business, do you know how many people went broke doing that? Your too late all the best claims are taken." In the music business, it is the same but framed a bit different.

Bless the true prospector and entrepreneur in the music business. These people gather the tools, have a good idea on how to proceed and where they are heading and what to do when they get there. I am talking about the grizzly old prospector who loads up his burro with a shovel, beans, gold pan, a wealth of knowledge and a whole lot of persistence. Inspiring artists must learn from these die-hard professionals.

One statistical trait that I have observed over the years in regards to aspiring artists is that many of them are focused on their own "Thing" way too much. In the process, they neglect to learn about the business they will be making a living in.

To make my point, I deliberately decided to survey everyone who said they are an original artist to see if my theory could be validated in respect to just basic common sense. Therefore, I asked each artist (including bands) "when was the last time you went to a major concert event?" The answer most given will most likely surprise you. Ninety five percent of the time the answer was basically, "It's been a long time or I don't remember." Frankly, this is an example of a huge "Dream Stealers." Unfortunately, most artists take the self-guided misdirected stance that robs an artist of the knowledge that they so desperately need. In just about any business learning and understanding the successes and failures of competitors is critical. The music business is a fiercely competitive business. It is interesting and the main reason why many budding and hopeful artist don't find concerts enjoyable is jealousy. Instead of enjoying the concert they find it difficult to separate the internal desire to be on that stage themselves. I personally have heard artists say on many occasions that it is upsetting to see others doing what they dream of doing. The confusion, pain and emotional stress it can create can deter many from learning from the best. However, this is not true for all artists. Some fully enjoy going to these spectacles of performing arts because they bring home new ideas and new burning desires. It is best to be the latter. The ones destined for success take home with them a renewed inspiration to work even harder to get the creative juices flowing. I believe every new band or hard working group should take regular monthly field trips to major concert events. This can either define a future or expose the flaws in the professional attitude that will eventually destroy the artistic process.

The old grizzly prospector knows he must search for gold in an area that has been proven to produce GOLD. The golden opportunity comes for any person who becomes inspired by others success and learns from their behavior and their attention to the details that makes success possible. Someone does not have to be the best out of the gate, but able to follow through with the established proven process.

Chapter 17
Live by the Ego, Die by the Ego

Over the years, I cannot understand artists that are early in their journey and still wet behind the ears yet think they deserve to be handed the golden ticket. If there is one trait that turns a music executive off it's when an unknown upcoming artist expects to be treated as if they have already packed 50,000 people into a stadium and sold 5 million records. Am I missing something here? Many upcoming artists have been told by so many people that they are fantastic and deserve to be a STAR, this starts them down the ego road. Although many are quite talented, for some reason all this uplifting and embellishment spills into the part of the brain that controls the basic human common sense mechanism and can become a detriment to success. There are good egos and then there are unhealthy egos.

Trust me, I am an advocate that all new comers and youngsters should be encouraged to strive for success but when this encouragement creates a selfish monster than this can become a serious problem. Not to mention destroying rare and important relationships and the possibly of acceptance into the club. Diva-ism and unfounded ego projection only goes so far before it becomes an undesirable characteristic. Where many artists go wrong they fail to understand this is not a "ME" business. The "ME" part is important when the artist is engrossed in the process of growing as an artist but when transitioning into the commercial world the artist must make the switch to the "You" business. The "Me" should stop once the artist begins relying upon savvy business people that invest their professional time, money and efforts into their "Dream and Future."

There are multiple "Dreams Stealers" that robs the talented individual from rising to the top of the music business. They are: selfishness, stubbornness and the obvious perception that the world revolves around "me" syndrome (WRAMS). Profound egos are only reserved for those who have mastered the art of pure professionalism, stellar accomplishments and understanding humbleness. I agree that ego is a strong part of all people who have strong confidence in their talents and abilities but when that same ego morphs into an un-likeable creature the game changes. The doors begin to slam. Eventually, no matter how good an artist they are they will find themselves burning all the bridges and find themselves alone and abandoned someday.

What most artists don't understand is, the individuals that have agreed to dedicate their time and money into forging opportunity for them expect a meaningful and truthful relationship. If a huge ego gets in the way it can cause unforeseen issue later down the road.

For example, I have a major record company executive friend that has told me about artists that "I could care less how good they are, their nasty behavior and egos are a joke and I would never sign someone like that again." If investors sign an artist, they want to feel good about their investment and be successful. They want to show off their new race horse to the rest of their colleagues. They too have an image to project and protect as well. Difficult people don't go too far in this business.

I believe this would be a good time to share a real-life story that will help describe the devastating effect of an out of control ego.

Not long ago, an incredibly talented artist from another country was discovered by a well-known brilliant Producer. After working with this artist for a short while it was clear that this was not just a good artist but a very rare talent. Before they knew it the artist was selected to be on a major national music performance reality show. For multiple weeks, the artist's flawless performances reduced the completion to just a few contenders for the final crown. This ongoing weekly spectacle quickly created a recognizable new artist. During the broadcast season when the artist went to the mall or in public the artist was swarmed by fans. You would expect this to be an exciting development in a new artist's life. Unfortunately, as you will see how this humble beginning could manifest into a misunderstanding of how to build upon success instead of internalizing and growing an attitude of "ME" resulting in a bad case of the destructive ego bug.

Now that I have your attention let us see how this turns out. Although defeated in the later stages of the television competition to everyone's dismay, the artist went on to perform at local events, gaining support and experienced a growing fan base. The artist released a new CD and video with some good results. All the time sucking up every bit of attention that could be gathered. Unfortunately, this was not enough, it was not moving fast enough so the artist decided that the world was next. Reminder, it has only been nine months since the airing of the first reality show episode.

Shortly thereafter, the artist contacted a United Stated based successful music executive to try to launch a career in the United States. Since the artist was such a timely and excellent new artist, the music executive agreed to pursue and see what he could do to find promotional opportunity in the US. This resulted in the artist traveling to the United States to explore a career in Hollywood.

If anyone knows anything about the music business there are tens of thousands of artist and bands competing in Hollywood, not to mention every other city in the US and worldwide. There are few opportunities to be accepted into the club of successful commercial artists. A commercial artist is one of those people who are being supported by a major commercial organization and the artist is actually making a living in the business.

It did not take very take long for this artist's ego to become such a problem that the excitement, trust and magic leaked out all over the floor. Consequently, the doors began slamming shut faster than they were opening. The artist had all the answers, demanded to be placed on a pedestal and would not take advice from anyone. A typical "My Stuff " does not stink attitude. Don't get me wrong, there is nothing wrong with having a strong belief in oneself but to exude the air of superiority can be a huge turn off to most people. Remember, no matter how good you think you are it is not your decision to rate yourself. You must humble yourself and fit into the family and go along with the program.

The result was, the only solution for the music executive was to send the artist back home. Sadly this particular artist drifted into oblivion never to be seen or heard of again. The sad thing is the people who originally invested their time and efforts into this artist were people who surely could have launched this artist's career to great height. Very sad. In the music business, great opportunities only come around occasionally. Therefore, at all costs, don't become someone else's nightmare because you believe the entire world revolves around you. The outcome will not translate into the result you are looking for.

Chapter 18
Reality Check. What Does It Cost to Become a Commercial Artist

So many bands dream of traveling from city to city, country to country in luxury tour buses and performing to packed arenas. There are other motives but let's just stick to these right now. As you know, I always ask bands seeking my advice questions to help paint a picture for them of the journey to come. Just like a leader of an expedition to the North Pole. My questions are designed to present the potential un-pleasantries and costs that are before them. I try to unveil the consequences of their decisions to pursue such a dedicated effort. Each of these examples can be used as a subset of "Dream Stealers" combined with and if not truly understood can burn up a great artist and band in micro seconds.

I try to get down to the basics and identity the primary roadblocks that can greatly influence someone's life in the music and entertainment business. These key "Dream Stealers" are related to: 1) Financial responsibilities, 2) Marital Status and other relationships, 3) Purpose, 4) Commitment to completion, 5) Attitude, 6) The willingness to take advice and sticking to the plan.

Financial responsibility and commitment can easily wipe out a hot budding artist or band. Most seasoned and experienced explorers fundamentally understand this concept because they all eventually start talking about requiring major financial support, investors and the preverbal front money. But unless they are accountants and managers this will never make any sense to them unless they understand the fundamentals.

To make my point and set the stage for the entire exploration into the depths of the artist's ability to accept and overcome the truth must be discussed. Starting with and asking the right questions beginning with:

1) Are any one of the members married or have long term relationships or have children?
2) Is everyone that has something at stake also 100% on board? Are they willing to sacrifice everything necessary to pull off their dream? Are they willing to stick with the program no matter what?

The looks on the faces of most artists usually says, "So what? What does this have anything to do with me?" Next Questions:

1) Do any one of you have mortgages, rent, car payments, car insurances payments, pay for medical insurance, have credit card bills, outstanding loans, child support payments, utility payments, etc.?

Finally, here comes the "Oh Boy" question.

2) Has anyone in the band ever been convicted of a felony?

This is an important question because if a key member of the band does it may be very difficult getting visas in many countries for touring purposes. Remember, I am talking about "Dream Stealing," so let us get to the substance that matters. Last thing anyone needs in the organization is to find out the hidden skeletons that can stop progress or cause huge and real problems in the future.

Only the strong shall read on if you really want to go on this journey.

I ask many similar insight questions to determine the strength of the foundation of any artist or group. Apply those questions to yourself. It is not the talent of the artist that makes for a good candidate to achieve success but their ability and desire to overcome the real-life obstacles that stops progress. Especially in this very difficult business. As a professional, I too must be realistic and talented enough to reveal these action items for focus, realignment, correction and further development.

I also want to enlighten the reader in regards to why finances steal most people's dreams in this business. To level the playing field, I quickly guide them to a profound sense of reality by first putting the ball in their court. I carefully let them know I could careless at this point about their music, art or alter egos.

Therefore, I ask, "So how much money do each of you need to just pay your bottom line expenses at home? That includes rent, payments, utilities, etc.?" I stress this issue because it is important.

We already covered this in Chapter 11 but this is important so we are going to talk about it again. We learned what the extreme touring costs are for a new band to stay on the road for just one year. Therefore, touring does not make long term sense with a new band or artist that has huge financial responsibilities. In this case these individuals would need to explore different approaches if these elements will create such a financial burden that it becomes almost impossible for a band or artist who are giving up their jobs.

What are you willing to sacrifice? What are you willing to do to offset the extreme costs associated with the journey you are planning? The best approach is to be ready to become a money making asset to investors from the start. Artists have to put the right entertainment value package together that is guaranteed to work out of the blocks.

The budding artist must understand the vast intricacies related to "Dream Stealing." If artists take the time to understand this it will help them to be more open minded and will make the right progress toward accessing the essence of their dreams. This book has only just explored a few true to life examples of what decisions an artist must make and the actions they must take.

The "Dream Stealing" effect on an artist's career is no different than the results experienced from a spike strip being thrown in front of a brand-new Ferrari going 100 miles per hour around a curve. The damage can be so complete that there may be no way back unless you start all over with a new vehicle. This can be very costly in time, patience and money. It can also cost your valuable relationships in the process.

I am sharing my life experience here so really think about, what is required of you and what is at stake. What will be the cost if you don't think about the consequences? If you don't keep your dream on the road and don't pay attention to the hazard signs ahead of you or don't listen to the telltale signs like a smoke detector that warns the "Dream Chaser" of impending disaster, then the odds of success are diminished.

Let me share a boiled down and concrete formula for success for you using the "One Fan at a Time Concept."

In building a successful business, it is important to know what it costs to acquire a new customer or fan. Major successful investors know how much it costs through promotional and marketing efforts to acquire loyal customers and keep repeat customers. You need to determine this for yourself. Playing out three or four nights per weeks, what does that cost? Promotion and Marketing costs, what else?

I would again like to share a real-life success story of an artist who took this concept to the next level and became extremely successful.

A very brilliant artist that I am acquainted with learned the costs and rewards of building a huge fan base. This artist was a smart musician and a good pianist. This artist was not someone you would expect to pursue a career in the music business but this unique individual knew how to build a loyal fan following. It was accomplished by mastered the art of turning "Dream Stealing" into "Dream Catching."

How this example of success was weaved should be a case study for anyone trying to accomplish the impossible. The discussion of these examples I provide in this book, if taken to heart, will give you the understanding of the natural process of this business. That is, if you just give it a chance to sink in. So, pay attention.

The strongest basic building block is the "One Fan at a Time" approach. Most artists don't have the fortitude for this, most want success right now. Don't fool yourself, nothing comes easy and everything is difficult. However, once you read the next example of this successful artist it may just turn on a light for you.

This artist along with his piano and a simple 8 track digital recorder and exceptional microphone turned into a multi-million-dollar business with loyal fans and loyal customers from all over the world. It was accomplished by following a well-defined process, dedication, persistence and a lot of stamina. A few years ago, the artist started by creating a CD of "seasonal" piano music to make s few extra dollars. Once the artist decided which music to record he began the many hours of practice required to perfect his performance. Most of the music he selected was from obscure but amazing classical compositions or old standard classics. Next an appropriate name was given to the project. Something catchy as "European Classics for the Winter Season" or "The Mountains and the Seasons." The artist then placed the fine microphone inside his grand piano and for the next month played and recorded each song. These songs would be played over and over until each recording performance was technically acceptable. The focus was on instrumental piano music only with no vocals or other instruments. We are talking the basics now not a big costly production evolving may different temperamental personalities. I remind you this did not cost much or involve a major recording studio budget, songwriting, a manager, agent or record company. The artist would spend about two hundred dollars and hire a graphics artist to do some simple artwork. No CDs were manufactured until the orders were in. He produced ten (10) technically correct mastered tracks and some simple CD artwork.

We need to back up a bit here, this artist's remarkable journey began when he located every hotel in his metro area that had a piano in the lobby. He contacted those hotels and spoke with the hotel managers. He simply asked if he could play the piano in the lobby for free in exchange for tips. Who in their right mind would not accept an offer like that? The artist also asked to be allow him to place a card on each table with a pencil that the hotel guests could use to write down their email address. This is what was printed on the card:

I enjoyed playing for you and I have an amazing new special edition CD being released soon and I would like for you be the first to have it. Please provided me with your email address and I will let you know when it will be available for only $3.00 each, my new CD would make great holiday gifts for this year. Thank you

Using this simple technique year after year he obtained thousands of email addresses. The artist remained in contact with his fans throughout each year to updates them on new projects. Around each September he would send out emails to the fans announcing the new CD project for the holidays requesting orders. To this day the artist sells between 250000 to 300000 thousand CDs each Christmas season for $3.00 dollars each. Netting him close to one million dollars a year. During the year, the artist continued to play at hotel lobbies, collecting more emails and gathering music for the next year's project. Each year minimal time was spent recording at home and repeating the process year after year. This is simply amazing and can be done by any artist or band. Open your mind to this type of thinking.

Your persistence, using your time wisely and spending the time to build your powerbase will create the future. All artists should learn to think in this manner if they want a sustainable and rewarding career. This is just one example of building a future "One Fan at a Time." Use it.

Remember the questions asked earlier. What can you do to overcome any obstacles that may be before you leave on your journey? Take time to think about it and prepare.

"The basic building block: One fan at a Time"

Chapter 19
They Don't Understand Me As an Artist

"They don't understand me as an artist." I have heard this statement so many times throughout my career I could just scream. I would like to know who "they" are. The records companies, Mr. Big, the high school football team?

The fact is, creative expression is a foundation for original new ideas. No artist should ever be deemed at fault for their original perspectives but there is a line drawn between commercial viability and creative stagnation. It is the natural path to create and be focused on pushing the limits. Consequently, for most artists who want to make a living in the entertainment industry they need to blend commercial reality with creativity.

There are bands that I have had the opportunity to work with that grasped this concept and ran to the bank with it. Most of these bands understood the concept of entertainment value not the throw it at the wall and hope it sticks concept.

One of these bands got disillusioned by the concept of competing in the original market and decided to become one of the best copy bands in the country. That is exactly what they did. They focused more on the entertainment value attributes that could be marketed worldwide than trying to create a new brand to express their creative original writing. For this group of musicians this made more sense than trying to complete for the last two remaining open slots on the records company's new investment roster for the year. Can't blame them. They have bills to pay, families to feed, and mortgage payments to keep current.

The fact is, there are countless more paying opportunities for cover bands than original unknowns. Why is that? This is because the public in majority are only interested in what they are used to and are familiar with. Therefore, keep in mind what original entertainment you decide to create better be something quite special. If you can create this familiarity with the masses, then you are "In." Imagine going to a traditional wedding where only original music is played. There is a place and time for it.

It takes a different animal altogether to compete and live in this ocean. This example is being presented only to make a point. A musical organization focusing on true entertainment can transcend many of the misconceptions of what is considered success or not. This is especially true when making a sustained living in the business, it is extremely important.

The current television network music reality competitions that are so popular these days clearly demonstrates the risks an artist is willing to take. These shows focus on unknown artists performing known copy material rather than original music. Why? Because the audience is more familiar with the material being presented. It allows the artist to focus on the performance not the song itself. Most audiences want to be entertained by familiar music they can relate to and can sing along with. If there were a show presented that focused completely on original music week after week it would last as long as a pepperoni pizza in front of a little league team after the big game.

Let's face the music, there are artists that are blessed at birth and are just naturals. It is almost freakish. They just "Have It." For us in the industry, we just don't try to understand. We find it fascinating and immediately start to find ways to take amazing talent like this to a world stage. I have been acquainted with artists with this amazing talent that don't want the life style or to achieve celebrity status. This is not their desire or goal in life but the talent they possess is stellar in commercial value. The question is, how to tap into this talent while not disrupting their life values. There are some unique options for these people.

Then there are the people who are not as talented and have the celebrity bug so bad that they never stop to think about the modification they need to make to give themselves a chance to compete. I fear these personalities the most because the pits of failure are full of these lost dreamers.

Over the years of great study and interface with countless successful and unsuccessful artists I have clearly identified and categorized certain traits and the probabilities of success for each of these specific individual personality types. These traits are based on people that are actively pursuing a career in the music industry or desire to achieve a level of success in the industry that may elevate them to celebrity status. Below are the buckets of the typical personality traits that most artists fall into. Which of these seven buckets do you fall?

1) Unbelievably Talented: Approachable, professional, humble, focused, respectful, open minded and confident.

2) Unbelievably Talented: Self-centered, moody, selfish, unapproachable, disrespectful and overconfident, uncooperative.

3) High Potential Talent: Humble, realistic, respectful, open minded, focused and dedicated.

4) High Potential Talent: Closed minded, somewhat professional, dated, know it alls.

5) Low Value Talent: Open minded, cooperative, confident, dedicated, aggressive and respectful.

6) Untalented 1: Aggressive, dedicated, persistent, respectful and inspirational.

7) Untalented 2: Emotional, sometimes delusional, unpredictable, unstable and aggressive.

Everyone has an angle, their own creation and the next best thing. After receiving enough CDs, tapes and promotional packages over the years I have learned to respect each and every one for their unique values. However, I feel I can speak for many of my industry colleagues as well as most industry professionals in that we only prefer to work with those artist and bands that fall into buckets 1, 3 and 5.

Each artist I have come across that is trying hard to get their foot in the door tries very hard to increase their chances of being noticed. I have great respect for that. Therefore, we must ignore the presentation quality of most tracks and promotion packages we receive. To find common ground we must overlook the low budgets invested in most submissions and listen and pay clear attention to the true intent of the artist. In many cases, some of the best material I have ever heard came from these resources in their raw form. It has always been a humbling experience to have to respond to an artist that I am not interested in their work. Really, who am I to judge? However, it is my job. Remember, for most commercial industry executives our goal is to make money for our stakeholders and the artists as well. This includes invoking a reality check on which creation may have a highest probability of success in each market or time frame. I wish I could have been given $1.00 for every artist that said to me that "I was full of garbage" in my evaluation of their material. But most artists must first understand and know what the industry is actively looking for to get a favorable response of, "I'm interested and I want to hear and know more."

The general misconception is, if you send out 1000 email presentations that surely someone out there will like it and will throw a record deal at you. In some cases, this works for only the ones that have done their homework. Even if the first efforts produce a favorable response this is just the beginning. With the invent of digital recording and extremely powerful computer plug-ins and software most seasoned music skeptic can be astounded of the quality of music being created. Believe me they are not fooled.

The questions that surely comes to mind when I like an artist or band submitting material:

    A) Is this a songwriter who is trying to get their music heard?
    B) Is this a band ready to hit the road for 10 years of hard work?
    C) What am I listening to here?
    D) What is the story behind the artist?

I ask myself these questions because I am interested. If a major investor were to be asking these questions what would you say about yourself to make them interested in you?

It is the prodigal cooperative artist that all executives are looking for, not the self-centered difficult "Me Me Me" artist that will not cooperate or is so difficult that they destroy their own future before your eyes. All industry executives want to get to the foundation of the matter and clearly understand the angle of how the artist is approaching their career. Without this clear understanding, how can one also buy into the complete package that is necessary to make it in this very difficult business? How do you protect your investment?

I am saying this so that you understand how you can change the events in the future when you try again to get noticed by the industry thus bettering your chances of success.

Like I said, I would prefer a borderline cover artist that has a clear focus on their market and wants to create entertainment value than a well-greased original artist that thinks they are in control of the universe's elements.

What is your angle, true entertainment purpose, baffle everyone with maximum volume, controversial lyrics, and focused intent, true artistic expression then expecting nothing in return? Is your angle about following the shirt tales of thousands of other artists doing the same music or breaking new grounds in the art of live performance? Does it matter? YES. If you think otherwise, then think again. It is important to understand what you are doing.

I know of a great band consisting of six members. They were some of the most talented group of musicians I have every come by. Their music flawless, their harmonies world class and each member could command the stage. What made them different is they were all 300 pounds plus. They mastered playing familiar music that people could identify with. I believe they were called "The Big Boys." They were one of the top demand bands around. They lived the life and became quite successful. They were smart and blended great music, entertainment, humor, personality and novelty into the holy grail of "Popularity." They had to turn down countless performance dates. This was their angle. They identified with their market. They did not compete with other bands, what they created was humble, natural and they stuck with what was working for them.

The fact, is someone in this business needs to want to be in the entertainment business. As I mentioned before, I am always respectful to all artists good or bad because they deserve the respect. Some expect too much and many don't give back enough.

Original artists are a different bunch altogether. In most cases they don't give themselves enough credit for their hard work. You may be one of them. It is an amazing phenomenon that a group of musicians will combine resources, spend all their hard-earned money, sacrifice countless hours in the process of making a CD of 10 or 15 original songs. These iconic representations of the heart and soul bleed out with every drop of sweat as if they were the offspring of the creators themselves. Their hopes and dreams are embodied in these disks and tracks. They are confident these creations will be a ticket to participate in the game of recognition or the world of satisfaction of creative intent. Once these projects are completed they are quick to spread them out across the music industry in hopes of gaining the attention of a sponsor or commercial support system. They are hopeful some producer or music executive will hear it and change their lives. Perhaps in todays saturated market 1 out of 10000 or perhaps 100000 will this actually happen.

This process continues over time, countless emails, mailings, promotional disks spread out to every possible opportunity to be found only to be left to deaf ears and an empty voice mail and email box. This can be very discouraging and damaging to the fabric of the heart and soul of the artistic organization. Due to the fact that no one may timely respond or the expected effect is not achieved can create all kinds of obstacles.

As I mentioned earlier, most artists do not give themselves enough credit and the time to squeeze the juice out of the original efforts put forth. Don't make this mistake, for this too is a "Dream Stealer." Unfortunately, if the expected response is not realized by the artist or band immediately they start taking a second look at their project as something unworthy and start to second guess their artistic works. They forget the hard work and effort they have made. You have heard this before, "they don't like it and we should try something else, we need to change our style to something more happening." Once this conversation starts the internal problems it causes can be so brutal to egos and relationships within the organization that the bottom falls out. Then the next thing to happen is the dominant creative members start blaming the others for not listening to them or not moving in a different creative direction that one of the collaborators may have suggested.

To make my point, what is the problem here? What was the intent of the project in the first place? During the process of making the record everything is fun and exciting, like a first date experience. The creative process is exciting, growing, stimulating and alive. When the project is done, this joyful experience stops and the only thing left now is what to do with this box of CDs that just showed up at the front door. If there is not a strong response from the people they look up to, then only the strong minded and flexible creator can save the ship from sinking. You have to go back and fix what is not working with your entertainment organizations intent. If a comedian uses untried new material on a new audience and it flops does that mean he is a rotten comedian? No, it just means he did not have it right yet and he didn't have the magic content. The same goes with musical artists and bands as well.

The first thing most bands do is run right back into the studio to cut new "HOT" tracks that surly will blow "them" away this time. They start the process all over again spending more money and time in the effort to get the same reaction. They never give their original creation a chance to live. Dr. Frankenstein had the right idea. Create the monster and give it a brain so it can live. The brain to any band is installing entertainment value into the mix. The project must be given a chance to work and live. Face it, all musicians, if you become a working touring band you will play the same 15 songs, night after night, week after week, month after month and in some case year after year. You must learn to love your creations.

Going out and recording CD after CD trying to hook onto the magic tune without a deliberate reason to create it in the first place in plain nuts. Are you getting the point? Making music to make music is not what drives the successful writer, singer, musician, producer or even a record company to become successful in the music industry. It is imperative you have your own angle to pitch and dazzle or to get excited about. Please don't make the mistake for not having a reason to exists in the first place.

Ask yourself, how many artists out of millions or contenders or even super successful bands remain in the spotlight for 10 years, 5 years or even 1 year? During the time you are on top it should be glorious, exciting, fun, rewarding, purposeful and realistic. Even with the massive exposure of hundreds of finalists on the network TV music completions can you even remember the names of 20 of them? No. So, don't expect the same life expectancy unless you redesign and reengineer new beginnings.

You must give yourself credit and give your creation a chance to live. If the major players don't respond, give them a reason to respond. Remember it is about commercial value to investors, the bottom line is the bean counter will influence your ultimate demise.

I am going to touch on a subject that most of the seasoned pros and tenured warriors fighting the battle to the top will find close and dear to them.

I find this subject something that I list as a "Dream Stealer Ogre" under the bridge ready to do us in at any time. Since most musicians and creative people know nothing about the business, legal matters and the mechanics aspects of the industry they set landmines all around them. Each of these landmines can be a devastating blow to their shear survival. They don't even know they are doing it. Most music and entertainment ventures start off with humble beginnings with bright futures, bright dreams and with an unwavering confidence. As soon as the decision is made to "Go Commercial" the dynamics change considerably. When a group of musicians get together and they share ideas, jam, contribute intellectually and artistically this becomes the mother of invention, the birth place of hit songs and renewed possibilities. Through this process these collaborators can become life time buddies or can become so problematic that they become nightmares no matter how good the music can be. This is no different than any other relationship filled with ups and downs that must be managed and worked on.

It is not uncommon to see one of the hottest performing band blow apart at the seams because of conflict over copyright ownership, artistic contribution or failure to agree on the fundamentals of what they are doing. They never consider at the beginning or meaningfully discuss how their interactions and attitudes can affect each member's future rights. These organizations have to fully understanding what they are doing and why they are doing it and understand how business, legal and mechanical realities influence their ultimate landing place. If the process is starting to look just like a party, then that is not going to get anyone anywhere. The last place to learn these lessons is when thousands of dollars are spent, promises are made, verbal and written contracts have been made, investments have been spent and a recording has been created. I cannot tell you how many times I have warned artists of these pending realities while looking me right in my eye then walk right into the propeller blades.

Let's look at a few examples of what this looks like in the real world. A band decides they want to take that "great new song" that they just put together and make a single out of it. They also want to use the track in a music video and then immediately release it on the internet. Because they are so blinded by the idea they jump right into the project, roll up their sleeves and go to work. They don't realize it but they went from humble creation directly into commercialization. What most artists neglect to do is decide the purpose of the effort in the first place? Why, feed an ego, have a death wish or have a desire to raid the rent money? Is it time to go for broke creating something that is not to become part of the bigger picture? The basis of this entire book is about focusing on the bigger picture. In the beginning of developing quality entertainment, the artist must identify the wrong activities, bad processes and practices and stop performing senseless mechanics that burn holes in the fabric of success.

Let us move over to the other way of thinking. The world where there are no songwriter collaboration agreements created, no discussion of ownership rights or anything else that matters to the bottom line. Just the sheer shoot from the hip approach. There have been more disputes over copyright ownership that have caused perfectly good friends to become bitter enemies. No one wants to transition to only focusing on winning a lawsuit than focusing on the original intent of the relationship in the first place. This is a simple example of a very lethal "Dream Stealer" for many ambitious performers. Is your organization really ready for this journey? Are you ready for taking responsibility of your future?

If a musical master gets completed and instantaneously everyone jumps into shooting a video, stop, wait a minute, who owns that video? What is it going to be used for? Now is the time to think about these things. It is true, many organizations have somehow found their way out of this gauntlet and became successful but these are rare situations that warrant further study and your full attention. Nothing is worse that waking up some day finding some video camera operator claiming creative rights on your finished product. This is because they claim someone in your organization verbally said they would be given creative ownership for a reduction in payment. Ouch! You just created a "Dream Stealer" by inviting an outside "creative" entity into your organization. Never proceed with expensive creative projects that can be tied to ownership rights until you have taken the time to agree in writing.

The chapter related to the parallels drawn between gold prospectors and performing artists holds true. All artists that have shown attributes of a golden future will surely attract the claim jumpers and opportunists feasting upon others work and accomplishments. Even during the gold rush, only a very few ever hit the mother lode. Some get a few opportunities and find a few gold nuggets but to hit the mother lode is rare. Same for the entertainment business. However, there are countless others that make their living off these amazing people. Just like the gold pan dealer, the general store and the tent maker, the livery stable, the saloons, hotels, mining equipment merchant and finally the bogus treasure map printer. There are countless people who are truly necessary to provide the prospector with the resources to even get a chance to prospect in the first place. You must be smart and pay attention when your back is turned.

The same parallel can be drawn within the music industry with CD pressers, radio promoter, producers, recording studios, web designers and countless others that only want one thing and that is your money or a piece of the action. If one knows this going forward, the artist can be prepared by utilizing the resources effectively to obtain the right tools before the prospecting even begins. The reality is if there is gold to be found it is most likely that all the good spots are already claimed. This is why you need to have a reason, knowledge and enough smartness to learn how gold is formed, what processes is responsible for depositing gold and look where others have not looked before. This may include learning from others who know the characteristics of the steps needed to load up on the profits. Why is it that everyone wants a gold record? Whatever the reason I find it fascinating that so many thousands will compete for a very few spots on the only ladder going up. The attraction of fame, fortune and the fantasy existence is so strong that no matter what the prospectors will not give up until the last breath. Unfortunately, many of these "Dream Chasers" return with barely enough to buy a ticket home. However, it is not the end, it really is just a new beginning. Taking the knowledge, reassessing their approach, identify the things that worked and experiencing the failure process can quickly turn a "Dream Chaser" into a "Dream Catcher." This can only be possible by learning from the "Dream Stealers" along the way.

The platinum highway starts here. Every manager, producer, executive and critic defines viable talent differently, yet most artist I have observed, interviewed and had the pleasure to work with have a difficult time grasping the right opportunities even when it is staring them in the face. This is not surprising since most artists and entertainers chose the "fly by the seat of their pants approach." No matter how much debate exists and no matter how industry executive deliberate about "what works" the inescapable facts remains: The most important asset in the hands of the striving artist is to stop second guessing themselves and trust in their ability to learn the ground rules and find the right help. Unfortunately, locating the right help, wisdom, support and professional experience can be difficult and expensive. One of the keys to success is based on trust and building a rich network of talented and experienced success miners to aid the artist in the journey.

Secondly, the artist must actively pursue new knowledge and education to the changes in the industry and learn from the successful mentors that have taken the journey before them. All talent needs honest coaching, encouragement and mentoring. Every successful entrepreneur has something in common, they at some point in time relied on wisdom, experience, common sense and dedication of a coach to provide them with the tools that otherwise would have to be learned on their own. This goes for everyone in the music and entertainment industry including producers, engineers, songwriters and many other countless other people. This is the link to success that is so often overlooked. Savvy successful artists and creative individuals have figured out that the alignment of their own knowledge though quality mentoring is essential to their personal development and perhaps even their very survival. This is especially true in today's ever changing entertainment industry. The lack of confidence is an obstacle in this process. Many artists get stuck in a rut that they would rather be left alone to learn and create on their own. The reality is that there are clearly defined techniques, approaches and principles that applies towards success with any professional skill. You just can't get rich with only one gold pan. Unfortunately, by not learning and applying these basic principles most artists tend to delay the process of gaining the right momentum to grasp success. It has been said that you have a better chance of getting hit by lightning than getting a hit record but if you want to get struck by lightning you best stand out in a rainstorm and hold up a lightning rod high in the air. This may sound stupid but these are just the facts. Lightning will strike those who learn how to attract the power and not hide from it. Yet my history of observation indicates that most talented people don't necessarily want to be managed or be moved like chess pieces without regard to their career aspirations or personal needs.

The beginning of the end come to those who sit waiting for the big deal to drop in their laps. Since every artist, creative person or performer is motivated by a unique set of personal values and goals it is clear that in the end success comes from the quality of the personal relationships between other aspiring professionals. If you want to go to the moon, it requires you believe in and trust the knowledge and skills of other pilots who have taken the journey before you. Most people have no problem jumping into a cab with a total unknown driver and trust them with their lives but reject any honest constructive input from extremely talented and experienced professionals. Focusing on the wants blurs the lines between what the needs are which ultimately are the nuts and bolts to accomplishing the goal. The needs are the framework to achieve the wants. Does that make any sense? Artists need time to practice, create, and have a well-defined purpose, a brand, a good lawyer, manager and mentors.

Most Independent artists I have met are like leopards, they choose to be crafty individuals that prefer to forge their own destiny. I disagree with this concept. In the music and entertainment business it takes an honest and dedicated support system, trust and strong relationships to thrive and succeed.

"Turn yourself from a Dream Chaser into a Dream Catcher"

Chapter 20
Promotion and Those Who Claim to Be Success Brokers

In this chapter, I will be very candid about an issue that each and every artist should seriously accept as a lesson of utmost importance.

It has never been easy to find that big break, that defining moment when all those thousands of hours spent start to show some promise. That moment comes when an influential industry executive shows an interest in your work. That first time that new song gets major airplay or your new music video goes viral for a few weeks or your last performance get a great response. This is the juice that drives the engine to the next destination.

What I have discussed above does not happen without relentless dedication to your art. Unfortunately, many artists become so focused on success that they make themselves vulnerable to be taken advantage of by crafty industry individuals. This includes licensed and unlicensed agents, managers, promoters, club owners, radio promoters and producers. They find opportunity to pitch their services to either actually help the artist to the next step or suck the life out of their future. On the other hand, there are extremely talented and resourceful individual in the same fields that can weave extremely successful careers. You will surely cross paths with these people early in your career especially when you start to become more successful.

I warn you, be careful not to sign any contracts that cannot be properly verified by a reputable attorney. You must find a good attorney that will ask the right questions and an attorney that fully understand the music and entertainment business. Before you sign anything verify the legitimacy of any person or business entity. Investigate their successes, background and history. Signing an un-vetted contract or making verbal agreements are more trouble than they are worth. A bad agreement can kill the heart and soul of an amazing band or artist. You will know when the time is right to sign a contract because you will just know it. Be a free agent for as long as you can.

But first, you must learn more about what makes the industry tick before you can truly see how the lack of understanding can turn the process against you. Don't give up your dreams and hard work to someone that does not have the undeniable assets and resources to immediately add to your progress or your dream. Don't become a victim of misdirection and smoke and mirrors.

As a strong case for example, magicians are the masters in the art of deception by using the limitations of the human sensory capabilities to create misjudgment or misdirection of perception.

These masters use lighting, sound and other falsehoods that confuse and distract our normal perspective into situations that our mind can only process in real time with un-altered reality. We wonder why we enjoy the art of magic. This is true because we cannot believe how easily we can be deceived. Unfortunately, this human characteristic flaw can be used for less than honorable means. If exploited properly most people never see it coming. Even though we pay close attention sometime we cannot see the deception. The only way to not be deceived and eliminate the misrepresentation is to learn more about the realities in the entertainment business just as if you were to learn the basics and principle of the magician's illusion. Once you know why and how the illusion works then the mystery is solved and awareness takes its place. Thus, the clarity and the misdirection become clear. You know what you want. Don't make the mistake and sell yourself up the river if you have something of great entertainment value that is ready to go. Don't allow yourself to be so needy that you will lower your defenses to invite others into your dream or be misdirected. Because once you let them in it is very difficult to get them out. I have seen so many fantastic artists slide into the grinder because of this one single event of trusting the wrong people or organization or signed a worthless binding contract with someone who cannot deliver. At all costs, do not make this mistake be careful with your future and select only the best help you can get.

Chapter 21
Your Creativity Will Set You Free

Who needs a major record company today when you have direct marketing on your side. No question major record companies have their place in the big picture. Today however, laser focused creativity and utilization of powerful technology can drill a hole in the once dominated and highly controlled corporate stronghold called the music business. Just trying to "break through to the other side" can become an exhausting effort even for the most talented and the highly dedicated. Success by design is the sure path to be taken. There are songwriters, and then there are songwriters by design. One creates to fulfill a desire to express themselves because this is a natural process, while the other creates for effect on others to generate a commercial viable product.

A few years back I was on a business trip to meet with a new client in a major US city and after a daunting day of playing the game of wit and intellectual posturing I was extremely tired and without much patience. I was dealing with a group of closed minded know it all want a be 'Me Me's" who lacked even the minimal knowledge of the fundamentals of the business. I questioned whether I could muster up the energy needed to start the same process all over the next day. I relied on my own instincts and experience to do what I do best and pressed on with keeping them on track. The truth is 99% of bands, performers, songwriters never make it to the starting block because they are more interested in what shoes to wear than focusing on the act of running a competitive race. I am always baffled about this form of thinking when it comes to new artists trying to make a go at it.

On my way back to the hotel I decided to pick up one of the local entertainment weekly newspapers at a deli and turned directly to the local live entertainment section. In this section were column after column of booking ads for dozens of local music venues and watering holes. In this city alone there were at least 400 bands and artists listed to perform during that entire month. Listed in this magazine was every cleaver band name you could think of: The Screaming Yellow Jackets, the Bee Boos, the Jerry Bob Band, XOXOX and a soup of other identities. Each band picture looked just like the one before.

Anyway, I decided to pick a few bands from the list and head out on the town to listen. This seemed like a good distraction after the long day I had.

I found myself in a smoky dive somewhere down town sitting by myself in a corner booth taking in the experience. After being subjected to a few punishing and sad performances I was pleasantly surprised to come across what I call a natural talent. They had it all together. I was impressed, (which for me is difficult) they were simply great. They all were great musicians, they all were quality lead vocalists and all played multiple instruments. They were simply amazing and exceptional entertainers. It was obvious they had a plan and they executed it flawlessly they knew exactly how to control the audience. I felt I did not pay enough money to see them. With them the $10.00 cover charge went a long way.

Once I got a chance to speak with them is was clear they understood what entertainment affect was. It was such a great breath of fresh air after what I was dealing with four hours before. This band was using their creative edge to set them free to explore, evolve and enjoy what they were doing. The patrons of the club just loved them. They were an example of how each new creative group or artist must perform and as if it were their last performance of their life. I would have signed them on the spot if I could have but I needed to get some sleep.

Every super successful Broadway show, TV series, movie sequel and book series has a final closing night, end or conclusion. The same goes for most musical performers, rock stars and idols. What residual impact is left behind is the real essence of the creation in the first place. Each artist must stop and at least be realistic to the perceived life cycle expectation of their creative effort. An artist that creates only one hit song can follow its affects through an entire successful career while others that create ten marginal albums with marginal presentation surely will dissolve into obscurity. The effect of the art is either designed for success or simply a mechanical process that is worthless

How valued do you want to be as an artist? This is a great question to ask yourself or if this is not important then it is time to order the local community college course catalog and start studying for another career path. A successful career can last for one project, one year or an entire lifetime. You do have a choice. It is only limited by your creative goals.

Let's draw a comparison between a person who was born with natural talent and decides this is the career path that must be undertaken. Either this person follows the path of most artists that are shooting from the hip or a well-disciplined person that knows how to create "valuable art." I have always wondered why many artists focus so much effort into burning the candle at both ends trying to have it all before they even get to step one. Creativity takes time and is a dedicated effort.

We all go to the movies and when we leave the theater we naturally do an assessment consciously or unconsciously. We ask ourselves, were we entertained or not? Did we make a connection with the intent of the creators? Did we get our monies worth? Do we want to see the sequel? This is how entertainment value becomes meshed with our expectations. The result of the creative effort can have a residual effect on the audience. If any artist falls short in delivering the full impact of what is expected, then the entire effort is essentially worthless. A flash in the pan. Careers are not made this way. Musicals and performing artists cannot become the equivalent of a "B" rated movie. They should be designed as a blockbuster from the beginning.

Songwriters are the first line of creativity in the music world. Many just have a natural ability to create. On the other hand, not all songs have entertainment value. Don't hang your future on marginal material. I assure you, every day of the year thousands of new songs are written by thousands of new artists. If you were to listen to all of them at once it would sound like radio static and background noise. It is imperative that the artist tune into the right frequency and target very specific results.

Not every new play that is presented in New Your City becomes a commercial success but the ones that do are a result of creative excellence. We live in a self-governing networking society and the major commercial entertainment organization knows it. If you see a movie or hear a band or artist that truly touched your entertainment funny bone you tell others about it, right? Let me share again some of my own experiences that led me to feel this way.

I have heard thousands of new so called "Up and Coming Bands" throughout my career. I do have to say when one sticks out you know it. I find great fun and entertainment in a well-planned and seriously focused tribute band. I am talking about a band of artist's that did everything possible to pull off a mascaraed with precision workmanship to CREATE the illusion of absolute replication and not a cheap imposter. You know everyone else in the room who sees them perform also recognizes the same. Their focus was on excellence in art and performance, and illusion making. This is why they were successful.

On the other hand, just because they may be great and popular today does not mean they should continue to do the same thing for the next 30 years. There is a beginning, middle and end to everything. Prepare yourself to evolve into something new all the time if you want longevity. When it is time to evolve then use the same principles you have learned here. Bands and most musical artists get wound up into their own satisfaction when they should be focusing on creating satisfaction for their unknown audiences. As I mentioned earlier, making fans out of unknown audiences is the ultimate goal. This is done by handfeeding potential fans what they expect and nothing less.

Look at your shadow, who is in there, is there just a dark and unrecognizable form or someone who's deepness is recognizable. Can you make your shadow perform and come alive? Or is it just another shadow that blends into all the others around them. This life expectancy of this shadow is only going to last as long as the light stays on. What is that light? Right? entertainment value and creativity. Once you stop becoming an entertainer only your residual energy and your years of work shall be all that is left.

This book is about "Dream Stealers" therefore I must cast my vote that the number #2 "Dream Stealer" is: When someone loses their desire to "entertain" and steps into the darkness and focuses only on other outside influences that distracts the artist from their destiny then their life-giving creativity starts to dim – their "light goes out."

"Look at your shadow, who is in there?"

Chapter 22
You Can't Please Everyone

I once had the opportunity to watch one of the hottest new artists destroy the opportunity of a life time. It was not just the fact that this artist killed one of the best possible deals one would ever imagine but in the process, destroyed the whole organization altogether. Again, this was another case of a very promising artist that slipped away into obscurity.

This artist was being heavily pursued by a major investment label. The label also knew this opportunity was good and proceeded with their standard approach to do their due diligence to determine if in fact their hunch was correct. They are always careful to protect their investment. Therefore, the label requested a face to face meeting with me and the key band members.

The meeting started with customary parading through the posh corporate offices to the formal meeting room lined with gold and platinum records. This made the eyes of the band members brighten to the point of toxicity. I followed behind keenly watching every move of the A&R executives as we made our way down the hallway. To me it was just the standard operating procedure to the inevitable psychodrama that was to shortly unfold. I call this the "Mr. Smiley

Phase." This is the phase when all the people involved are at their best behavior hoping that they are about to bag a huge deal.

In comes the A&R Director who is there for only one purpose, to evaluate and determine if the meeting would move forward to the "Let's Meet Mr. or Ms. Big" phase. The point of this story is to show just how important focus and purpose is to an investment minded organization then the emotional investment the artist has that only cares about their own existence.

As we moved on, some pleasantries were exchanged and the small talk was over the A&R representative asked the "Artist" so "What exactly is your plans for the next 4 years?" The swift answer blared out from the band, "we want to go to Europe and a major label can do that for us. We have plans of writing and recording music that has a broad appeal for everyone." The band did not even mention the CD project that was already done which attracted the label in the first place. The looks on the faces of the label staff were solid and un-phased, no smiles. I just about choked. I am sure the next question was well designed by the label to determine if the meeting was to even continue. The director then asked, "Our producers have looked over your material and have their own ideas of a good direction for you and your next album, would you be open to working with them? The band leader said without a pause, "No thanks, we have my own producer and if we do a deal with you he will be my producer." The label representatives slowly stood up and looked me in the eye and said, "thanks for coming to see us today, we will be in touch." They then walked out of the room. The receptionist shortly thereafter escorted us out to the main lobby.

Needless to say, the label refused to take phone calls. The band was never heard from again. The lesson here is the investors need to protect their investment, market and are keenly tuned into doing everything they can to maximized their chances of success. All the answers given that day were well discussed with the band prior to the meeting but for some reason, as in most cases, bands and artists do not take the advice of their managers and advisors and act without common business or professional sense. "Dream Stealer" Alert!!!

Let us discuss this situation. When a band or artist is being pursued by a legitimate label it is prudent to understand you are being given an opportunity to become part of that organization's team and business plan. They plug-in the needed parts to make their plan work. Remember, it is about commercialization, marketing, and planning that gets a band or artist to a successful level not just the artists dreams, philosophy and expectations. There is no question a band's or artist's uniqueness is important but when a major investor label is involved the game changes dramatically. It is no longer about the artist. Therefore, when a band or artist closes the door and say "NO" in regards to cooperating with the label then they might as well go back to the computer and try a new viral marketing idea that 250,000 other bands just tried last week.

A band or artist can only appeal to a very specific and narrow market, never to all audiences. Labels are focused and not concerned that much with changing their business models. They gear everything they do on narrow focused demographics. If the artist is primarily a Country Rock artist, then that artist will never appeal to the Blue Grass buying market in the numbers that make it worth a commercially supported investment. Therefore, when an artist thinks they can be eclectic and can play all kinds of music and wants to please everyone then 99% of these people will get the boot out into the lobby area. Would you waste your time? If the label wants you to work with their staff, then you open the door to meaningful discussions and become part of the team and the family.

Too many artists and bands think they have all the answers. They think they hold all the cards and stick their heads in the sand. They think it is wrong to listen to the other side's great ideas and or plans for their future. These labels know their business. They might have great ideas. They might have a golden song from a writer siting in a special golden box pegged just for you that could be career changing. They might have a producer for which everything that this person touches turn to gold. If you have something special about yourself that is opening amazing opportunities than understand this is your spark in the darkness. Don't blow your light out because you think you have all the answers and you alone will please everyone. This business does not work this way.

If you play for two thousand people as an opening act and you do your absolute best, then just accept the fact that perhaps only 200 people may like what you are doing. This is a very good return on your efforts. If it is your plan to work with commercial powerhouses, then be cooperative all the time because today you need them to launch your career to millions. If you don't or are not willing to understand this very important concept and you persist in believing you can cover all the bases all the time, then it's time to get a career check-up and get your head examined in the process.

"Don't blow your own light out"

Chapter 23
Listen and Take the Advice Of Your Seasoned Advisers

Because you are reading this book it is a good sign you are moving in the right direction. You are educating yourself and I commend you. You are more likely to make your way thought the dark with this little candle than most of those who are closed minded and prefer to stumble around bumping into walls. This chapter comes from the heart of all the entertainment managers in the business.

It is to your best advantage to stay focused on the process of doing the things that are proven to work but at the same time allowing your individual artistic contributions to round out your future. Most of the seasoned mentors you will meet think like this and there is a reason for it. Be patient with them and open to all possibilities.

If you are a business or personal manager or producer, my respect for you is endless. You have one of the most difficult jobs in the world. I was asked once, what is it like to be a manager of a successful artist or band? My answer is "it is like trying to maintain six girlfriends all at the same time."

I am always on my toes to absorb information whenever possible. It is imperative that this information be relayed to the artists anyway possible. I am looking for the keys of success that most successful music professionals and superstars have to offer. Most budding artists tend to ignore what they can learn from seasoned professionals and attribute their success to some flash of luck or derived mechanical process. There are no rites of passage in this business. However, the fact is that success in this business is simpler than they think.

So here is some more good advice. If an artist wants to become a sustained success they must create something that people will remember and get excited about and sharing it with others. This is how this book got written. I got excited about sharing my years of experience with others. When you create something memorable it induces natural affinity for your fans to return for more to satisfy their musical palettes. Knowledge and advice have the same affect if applied properly. Once you start applying the knowledge given to you by reputable mentors and you start seeing the right changes in your life, only then will you be more open to additional advice or taking more direction. This is how futures are created.

Too many artists truly believe hanging out and hobnobbing with record company executives is going to give them the break they need. This has nothing to do with it. If this is the belief that motivates a budding artist, then this may prove to be a grave disappointment. Artists needs to be realistic in evaluating themselves to determine if in fact they have something amazing that will attract quality people to drive their career. A serious success oriented artist must understand, if you are lucky to find others with great management, production and business skills that are willing to help then invite them into your world in a real and honest way. When the chips hit the floor and failure becomes the flavor of the day don't blame these same people. This is never a good thing to do. The success rate in this business is small. Maintain and keep working with those professionals that continue to believe and support you through the dark hours.

When I decided to write this book, it was out of love for the music business, the thrill each time I experienced a truly professional concert or performance that left me speechless and wanting more. As a musician, myself, the thrill of the performance is everything dreams are made of. It is not hard to understand why so many people (young and old) want to take the ride, be part of the fun and be free to live the life. Each and every one of those people who become stellar music professionals knows it did not happen by accident. They each are a product of their efforts, dedication, vision, purpose, creation and other investment of time and money. However, over time each artist learns the truth and the skill of working the ropes of their sailing ship. This is the only reason why the journey is completed. It is always a blessing to have a great crew and focused leadership as well.

The basic foundations of success in the music business also includes:

A) Possessing the natural ability to want to entertain.

B) Having the true talent at which to create viable entertainment value and successfully evolve with the changes of time.

C) Maintaining a true and unfettered professional attitude towards success.

D) Being aware that longevity in the business is influenced by many variables that may be out of your control but can be managed with common good business sense.

E) You are not the center of the world but part of the dynamics of a well-defined business opportunity.

F) Trust in honest and sincere advice from the professionals that commit a vested interest in your future success.

Chapter 24
The Career After the Career

Most closed minded struggling and inspired artists believe once they make it to a somewhat successful level, (professionally or financially) the magical journey will last forever and the money will pour in endlessly. The truth is very few make it past their first uploads or first local tour. That is unless they make a huge splash with national exposure. However, those who pass the test of fire are rewarded for their efforts and achieve the next level. This affords them the financial well-being and balance they are looking for. Count it is a blessing. The battle of maintaining that success and the associated financial stability becomes with an investment of serious planning, common sense, dedication and appreciation for the privilege to be part of that world. If an artist loses a grasp of any of these attributes, then the long painful slide to "Startsoverville" begins.

Nothing will steal your dream faster than not having a financial and career plan in the event of a major success. Believe me, all the "do this and do that-ers" will crawl out of the woodwork and try to influence every move you make and where to spend your money. They will attempt to write your life's story for you. These can be attorneys, managers, record company executives, investors, family and friends. Really, what is your plan in the event that you breakout? Ever thought about that?

The music and entertainment business is unique when it comes to the earning potential one can achieve quickly. Earlier we discussed the costs of putting a touring band on the road. However, what we are talking about now is the strategy for up and above the initial start-up. If an artist or band hooks in with a series of hits on the radio, internet or otherwise, the rise in popularity can increase just as fast. The rise in popularity makes the earning potential increase proportionately. A band who is used to making 0 or $500.00 a gig can find themselves being transformed into $5,000.00 - $10,000.00 per show which then can increase to $20,000.00 - $40,000.00. What are you going to do with that money? Just blow it on garbage and waste it away? The gravy train may be in the station right now but may never stop at your station again. This is a reality you must anticipate and plan for.

Before you do hit the big time, you had better have all your financial affairs figured out in advance. This includes all of your agreements with bandmates, producers, investors, songwriters and co-songwriters and anyone else that has their fingers in your cookie jar. You need to think like a professional and someone who wants to be around for a while and financially secure after the end of the road comes.

I am discussing this because the facts are, there will be an end of anything good in this business 95 % of the time. It is best to play the odds and be careful with your future. Don't get me wrong, it is great to hit the bigtime but the bigtime has its problems to. Certainly, enjoy yourself but don't be stupid with your recently acquired wealth. When the money rolls in it starts to roll out just as fast. What if you could take a ride on the success popularity train for 4 years and then when times change you have everything you wanted out of your dreams and efforts. Wouldn't it be nice to walk away with enough to perhaps last you a lifetime? This is possible in this business.

The secret is when you are making hordes of money you don't spend it on anything but what is absolutely necessary. I assure you and I repeat myself, because of the nature of this business and when you least expect it, the gravy train will blow its last whistle someday. Just be safe. I hope you are prepared for its effect on your life and I hope you prepare for this situation. What do we call not planning for this eventuality? Right! a "Dream Stealer."

What is sad, I have been around and worked with many artists who have busted through to become huge earners in the height of their careers. These same people ended up broke or in financial difficulty soon after the record sales dropped and booking became less in demand. I remind you, there are other support staff in the organization who also depend on the same to survive financially.

These other people have no control over the outcome in regards to their future goals because it is attached to your stability and financial security. This can cause a whole different set of problems for the stability of the group and the group's future.

The key is to be smart here. Spending all the money on expensive luxuries, expensive food, travel, cars, toys, gift, parties, etc. will leave nothing for the future. If an artist or band cannot follow-up with a new successful project, then the money well will go dry and that will be the end of the once successful organization, guaranteed.

I have seen and admired a few individuals that were lucky enough to hit the mark in a big way. Their huge growth was like I expressed earlier. One of the members of this particular band was extremely conservative with his earnings. He knew that it would not last forever. He did not spend his money on worthless and impulsive things or wasted his hard-earned money on anything. Then the peak happened and the slide began and the organization revenue dropped greatly. In the end, most of the other members had nothing to show for their hard work and became desperate in many ways. They tried to resurrect the success but it would not catch on. Each band member had to make a choice on what to do and eventually the organization died a slow death. Many of these members during the ride up the mountain started families, bought and opened mortgages on nice homes and other material responsibilities. However, the one band member who predicted the very outcome had saved a considerable amount of money and purchased a series of sub sandwich shops and invested into start-up manufacturing companies. Today he lives a comfortable life making a great income.

They hit the motherload together, one miner saved his gold nuggets until the mine went bust. In the meanwhile, each of the other miners spent the newly discovered wealth down the hill at the saloon, gambling hall, bought fancy clothes and other luxuries to satisfy their immediate desires. Now the first miner owns the saloon, the bank and the general store and half the real estate in the valley. Listen to what I am saying here!

Plan on it happening this way if you hit pay dirt. If you are lucky to hit it huge, huge, huge then this is good, but it will require a bigger effort to work with tax accountant, tax attorneys, and others to plan your sound financial future. But you make the choices and decisions. Don't let others do it for you. You write the checks and keep it that way. Nobody spends your money more wisely than you do!

I hope you do hit it big. Your life after stardom can be just as wonderful and rewarding as the music journey itself. Think about what you want to do after your musical journey and start planning it right now with as much passion as you did with your initial music adventure. Dream again and visualize the future after the party is over.

Everything that does go up does come down. It is just a matter of how far down it goes. You need to know when to hold your position and when jump off the dream train when it comes to losing your financial future. Everything in this business has an end. Even for the superstars in many cases.

Start building a safety net at the exact time that you hit the big time. Don't make the mistake I described. A good thought is, if you play it right you will give yourself financial security and allow yourself once again the option to take another stab at the musical journey. This next venture would be on your terms, not from a position of being desperate. You will be able to take your time and do it right once again on your time and with an open and satisfied creative mind.

"Hit the big time, build a safety net"

Chapter 25
You Can Die From Too Much Exposure

No matter what advice is given to a band or artists the battle to help them make sense out of the unknown is always an uphill climb. The goal of ultimate success has its roots set in the foot prints of the pioneers of the past. What worked before may not necessarily work well in today's world or during any future time frame.

The artist needs to open their minds to new possibilities and advanced thinking that adds to the concept of entertainment value. I would like to express my views to the open minded here in regards the subject of "exposure." No matter what, "exposure" needs to be defined clearly and must be understood by the artist. The right understanding of the effects of exposure can become a limiting factor to the process and activities that drive the success factor further up the pole or results in the act of sheer survival.

Exposure can be good and bad. Presenting a new band, album, or any other commercial presentation at the wrong time can have negative repercussions that may never be repaired. For example, many bands and artists are so crazy to get out an album or play out in front of audiences that they rush the process or come to the battle ill prepared. This unsteady thinking leaves them venerable in a very high degree to the "you only get one chance syndrome." If you rush into the frontier without the proper equipment, knowledge and preparation it only takes one cold winter before the journey is over. This same mind set also goes with the entertainment business.

As mentioned earlier in this book, exposing yourself to a major label and not being technically ready to do so will certainly kill your chance for an open invitation of the same opportunity. One may say all exposure is good. I disagree with this completely and don't be fooled. If your goal is to perform for fun, then that is another thing all together. I am hopeful that you are reading this book for a reason to become successful in this business. Therefore, let's address the right attitude towards "meaningful exposure" verses going through the motions and the "hope it sticks exposure." We will explore something most artists don't want to talk about.

Let's not forget the hundreds of hours spent in the studio rehearsing and working on what most bands and artists believe are the most amazing songs ever. Actually, they could be. Let's not forget the thousands of dollars of rent money spent on top of that. Reality hits home when this music is played for new audiences and the performance is so boring and unmemorable that the cap of the pen hooked to the email list does not even get removed. This type of exposure is not the exposure any band or artist wants. This is one colossal "Dream Stealer" and not to mention it can also be just down right demoralizing.

In the context of this subject thus far let's look at the basic definition of exposure. This is essentially helpful in defining exposure as it relates to the entertainment business and artists alike. I see it as: "An act of subjecting or an instance of being subjected to an action or an influence, appearance in public or in the mass media, a new revelation or the act of being exposed to forces of nature."

All artists must grasp they may be playing the same songs repeatedly until the colors start coming out of the material. We all like something bright and new. Why should we not include the creative process in this situation. Just like anything else the colors start to fade the shine starts to dull and the surface starts to lose its luster. Remember this, it is not your choice if your creations are losing their initial power. It is your buying public that shall make that apparent to you. Just because your music is not getting the response you want does not mean that if exposed in a different geographical location that it can't again blow up into another super success. Be proud of what you created.

It is exciting while hot is hot and on a first tour, playing the same songs is part of the game. But over exposure in a focused area for a new band is dangerous. Living and operating in the same community for long periods of time will take your energy away. Really, how many times can you watch that same DVD even though you like it. The same with major movies that only stay in the market for only so long. The same goes with bands and artists. Their current presentation and show has a very defined life cycle if not exposed to other new markets. Creating a local success certainly is a great place to start but if you are doing the same thing for three years there is something very wrong with your overall marketing plan. All great smart artist and producers are hopeful and strive to create new enthusiastic fans out of new audiences. The life blood of a successful artist is when announcing a new album or tour and their loyal fans have no problem filling-up the royalty account with money. But if you give your following the same old set or do not vary your creative approach then this will slow down the momentum that you need to make it up the next hill under your own power.

Chapter 26
The Gifts Are All Around, Open Your Eyes

Recently, I had the opportunity to be invited to a local music industry seminar being presented by a prominent university. I was invited by the organizers to potentially lend any suggestions that may help improve their goals of developing a quality opportunity for their students. I agreed to be available but tried to stay a bit undercover just so I could fit in and not get cornered by bands and artists that recognized me. I just wanted to enjoy myself. There were obviously artists and creative people that came to learn something. Perhaps they were there to learn little tidbits that would change their life. Maybe they were looking to meet that one person that would take an interest in them or walk away with that magic twist that would open their mind to something new. They were surly there looking for a match to light the fuse to launch their rocket to stellar heights.

I found a comfortable place and listened to the panel of speakers who obviously had some standing in the music industry (booking agent, event manager and editor for a local entertainment magazine). I found myself analyzing the real impact that these individuals were having on the seminar attendees. I was quick to notice something positive was missing. Where were the good stories? Where was the inspirational information being shared that would spark a creative person to get excited and try new things? Everything discussed was mechanical. How to submit a promo package, how to get bookings, how to promote the band. There was no talk about the best way of thinking and or how to design solid success. There was no real mentoring going on. From the beginning the technical discussions and music business regurgitation only drove the same old train down the track to nowhere.

I respect the efforts of the university for putting on the seminar but the music business is more than how to present and create promotional material. It is a way of life and internal journey that has no boundaries. These boundaries must be explored for the creative power to be released, dedication is forged and long term meaningful collaborative creative and artistic relationships are started.

I must admit after the seminar I enjoyed being introduced to many fine and wonderful people by the organizers of the event. I immediately decided to see what I could do to make what was left of the evening a bit more special.

I thought to myself, let's try the Star Mentor's Approach. It is always said in this business that all the real substance of value happens after the meeting. This is where I feel most comfortable to work with inspiring artists. After the seminar, I was asked to come to a local watering hole where many of the attendees were meeting up to socialize. As I entered the room the seminar organizers introduced me to a few budding artists. I looked around the room and saw what might be a good group to get to know better and ask some probing questions.

Let's pause here for a minute. If anyone decides to change their future into something positive, it can happen at any time and at any moment just by taking the time to do so. Changing your life for the good, why not, there is nothing wrong with that. Why not change your life and make it to the top of the music business? You must decide it so. There are so many "Dream Stealers" all around us 24/7. Why not facilitate a better way of thinking by following the right path for your career and avoid many of these pitfalls and quick sand? Change your thinking process into a fresh new concept and make this journey matter. Don't fall into the trap of following the same old path of others. Go on this journey for real. Much of what you have already read in this book, if applied with the desire to succeed, should help you see there is a real opportunity for you. Don't settle for the mechanics of what you are doing. There must be an emotional and human component that you must embrace and energize.

In my career, I have meet many very special artists who are true to heart musicians and entertainers. They've always had that special magic in their eyes, respectful attitude, humbleness and professional qualities. What I have learned is that they all have something in common. They all have the ability to pay attention to the world around them. This is a defensive instinct essential to survival in the entertainment industry. Being aware of the world and life around provides the elements to create and finish the picture. If you take the time you might be surprised what you will experience or notice around you and how music and art can change your perspective even if for a few minutes.

That being said, I am sitting here right now on an airplane writing this chapter of the book with my head phones on listening to some of the most amazing music ever recorded on the planet. I happen to be sitting on the aisle seat next to a young lady in the window seat with her 8-month baby. She was playing with her baby, showing him things in a book, showing the sights out the window, smiling, laughing and lots of kisses were being shared. What is special is that when you have these amazing headphones on listening to this amazing music and watching the moments of life playing out you could swear it was a movie. I was watching a perfectly well scripted movie. All I needed was a sound track to see through the filter of reality around me and the illusion was complete. The fact is, you must be observant of everything around you to see the beauty and creative opportunities available to you. Opportunities are so abundant that one must stop for a minute and appreciate life for what it is and become part of it. The music business is the same in many ways but for you to notice the opportunities you must stop for a minute to decide what affect you want to have on the world around you. Once you do, you must create every opportunity to avoid the "Dream Stealers" at all costs. You need to apply the soundtrack of your life for others to experience the same when you are in front of them performing.

I want to take you back to the music industry meeting that I was describing earlier. I started to talk to one of the band members about their efforts to promote themselves. I admit I really was enjoying the interaction. I noted that other artists and their friends were listening in on our conversation. They started to join in and before you knew it there were many dozens of artists commenting and engaging in the conversation. We discussed alternative marketing strategies for bands and creative live performance. We were having our own seminar after the seminar.

The experience for me was exciting. Watching these budding artists learning and absorb different concepts, opening their minds to a different way of thinking. I must say, what happened during the next hour was what I hoped to see happen at the seminar, not just talk about the basic music business mechanics. I am sure the inspiration from that evening was key in my journey to writing this book. If you pay attention to these gifts of insight and creativity that are all around you, it will change you. When you look into the eyes of an inspired group of individuals or artist that understand this it is proof that anything is possible.

A few weeks after the seminar, I received a note from one of the artists that I was talking to. They told me that their band was trying and applying exactly some of the options we discussed. I will never forget the intensity of their undivided attention, the thirst to learn some different approaches that are unconventional in this mechanical minded cliché industry. Just the fact that this group of budding artists would take the time to thank me for the different perspective I presented I knew that I was right and that there is a defined path to success. You can make your mark in the industry if you want, but always remember this is a no nonsense business. Keep things simple and don't make it so complicated that you get stuck in the mud of technical stagnation.

"Changing your life for the good, why not"

Chapter 27
The Great Song Graveyard

There are song writers and then there are "Real" song writers. This "Dream Stealer" sinks more artist than anything else. There are artists that are just blessed for whatever reason to be able to assemble thousands of notes and beats into magical arraignments that penetrate the soul. They have the uncanny ability that can make audiences beg for more. They have the natural voice speaking to them that generates hit after hit. They just got it.

These people have something special and it should be just accepted for such. They accomplish this by either gaining the knowledge of how to write hits or just gifted in such a way that defies explanation. Regardless, their efforts and focus are simply based on true creativity, the power of observation with either lyrical messages or fundamental play with music, beats and melodies.

There are tens of thousands of bands that are created and destroyed on an annual basis. There are over 300,000 new songs uploaded on an annual basis to music distribution websites, typically by independent artists. The numbers are simply mind-blowing.

This being the case, most artists base their existence on the belief that their music is much better or more unique then the next band.

You really can't blame this behavior since competition is the underlying factor that rules the commercial music industry.

Most bands and artists assemble their forces and head out to the local clubs and concert halls to complete for the top spot. However, only the true artists assemble their musical existence on something from the beginning that has the basics for success. Nothing is more disturbing for me as a music executive minded person to listen to a series of bands at a local watering hole and hear the same music played by different bands. The same old let's throw it out there and see if it sticks approached. In the process, if confronted by these bands they usually ask me "Did you like it," "What do you think?" A well prepared and polished band should not have to ask those questions. They should already know how good it was. If they are purposely asking for suggestions that is something completely different. But most don't want to accept constructive criticism and that is not what gets an artist to the finish line to accept the a gold record. A confident artist should never have to ask those questions.

Let us back up and look at this subject more closely. Ninety percent of artists and bands see themselves as competitors. Some work for musical excellence and don't care about this mindset. Some artists accept the fact that there is a reason for even belonging to a group of temperamental individuals with different goals in the first place. While others should just quit while they are ahead because the polar ice caps must melt before they will ever realize their dreams. This is because the basic building blocks for success are just missing from their attitude about quality songwriting. An assessment must be made. We are talking about "making" a sustainable career in the music and entertainment business here. We are not addressing the hobbyist's reasoning.

Over the years, I have received thousands of CDs and track submissions. I have listen to thousands of the most popular commercial recordings in the marketplace and like everyone I have my favorites. My favorites may be vastly different than anyone else's. There are thousands of CDs that were professionally recorded that are amongst my library of historical archives that have never been released to commercial use, never got airplay or distributed. In most cases, never have been heard by anyone except for the original writers closest associates. In some cases, some of these amazing unknown recordings were written by those blessed unknown songwriters we are talking about. These creators, bands and artists could have been decimated long ago, fell apart or succumbed to many of the classic "Dreamer Stealers." Some of these amazing people left behind gold and precious gems just for the open-minded creative performer to reach down and pick them up, dust off the nugget and breathe life into an amazing songwriter's vision.

Why not be open to the concept of picking up gems and nuggets that were lost to the world in the past? Do you want to launch your career in a reasonable amount of time? Why not be open to the concept?

Some bands have the most talented technical players ever, but song writing is not in their skill set. It is a sad thing to witness the death rattle of a talented artist that succumbs to the "We only play our own music" syndrome. Sadly, their own music may be substandard to launch an artist or band.

Since the 1960s it is not inconceivable to estimate that there probably have been fifty million songs written and recorded into demos and sent out to record companies, radio stations and other music sites. The original masters surely are now in bottom drawers, basements and garages worldwide. There are countless hits hidden in those dark cold places. The gold miner must sort through thousands of tons of rock to find the jewels and precious nuggets. What is the difference for the artist who cannot "write hit songs", a miner who cannot make gold but they can find it? Remember, I am talking to the open-minded person here to help create options for success. Listen clearly to what I am sharing here. If anyone wants to have the proper tools in this business to do the job, they need to be open to the materials that will give them the edge. If a musical organization cannot write a hit song then hire a great songwriter, buy a license, find previously created songs and re-record it. Find what works for you to give you the "It" you need to make a huge impact.

Who care where it comes from. If you have great players it can change your life forever.

"Dream Stealer" Number 641: Don't put out contrived, marginal and senseless material. Many bands just don't have the right songwriting skills and should consider scripting their existence. For those that have these incredible skills, skip to another chapter, or not while I drive my point through to those who are struggling with this dilemma.

When movie producers are looking for music for their movies they usually select music from libraries of thousands of masters. They purposely select what works for the movie. They don't care who wrote it. They select scripts that meet their needs, they don't write them from scratch. Some hire the truly blessed proven composers and writers if they want to custom design a soundtrack. Any artist that must make an impact should always think in the same manner. Why do bands and artists insist only their music is the Holy Grail and are willing to turn their heads away from other gifted songwriters?

Here is some food for thought. Let's take a song, a fantastic song from 1983 or perhaps 2013. This song was written by a totally unknown band or songwriter. This great band broke up years ago because they became victim to a "Dream Stealer" and did not survive it's poison. They recorded three great CDs, never got signed, never got airplay and never got the right exposure. The songwriting was over the top, true excellence. When the band was around, every time the band played live the crowd when wild. There was something special there.

Let's run the time clock up a bit. Each member of this band now has a family and massive responsibility that has set in years ago. Each of these individuals now work professional jobs, own businesses and are simply doing what they need to do to take care of their families and meet their financial responsibilities. The breakup of the band left their songs dead years ago in a dark cold place never to be heard again. Those songs have officially been sent to the graveyard of 10,000,000 songs and buried eight feet under. The head stone bears the words "Here Lies One of the Best Songs Ever Written but Will Never be Heard Again." These great hit songs may never be heard again because the EGO of most bands and artists restricts the life of the magical song from being resurrected and brought back into the light.

Really, what about this buried music? This material can be "priceless" to the song prospector with an open mind to engineering success in the entertainment business. There are also excellent songs recorded and released by some of the top bands and artists in the world. An artist or band with the proper selections can add to their band's set that will blow the doors off the competition in the marketplace. Reader, open your minds to the possibilities here. It is about designing success ground up.

This is the entertainment business, not the ego driven "look what I created" world. What goes up does come down and any way an artist can keep the balloon up in the air the better their chances are that a brand can emerge allowing for more creative liberties in the future. This allows the freedom of the artist to emerge. You will be amazed what is under those headstones.

Dig some of them up and make them yours. It will accelerate your ability to do what you are trying to accomplish. Waiting around for the magic song to jump out of the bag or to be written by your organization may never come in the time frame you are allowed before the "Dream Stealers" show up to the party.

"Dream Stealer number 641: Don't put out contrived, marginal and senseless material"

Chapter 28
Lightspeed Track to Success

Each plan of success comes from following the right course. I always looked at the music business and success in it as a very defined and acted upon series of events meticulously prepared and expertly executed. It is not just putting up your ships sails and letting the wind blow you around. It is about how you set your sail, the way you use the wind to your advantage. Finally plotting the right direction to bring you to your destination in great condition. All success is by design. Sure, there are success accidents, but you must forget the luck factor right now which is foolish thinking.

It all starts with setting the success date. This is a calculated time when all the details of your plans are completed and the job is complete. That's right did I say "JOB?" If you accept the job, then it should be treated as one and therefore the work needs to be done. What date will your performing group be ready to compete on a solid professional level? If your desire is to win the Daytona 500 then ask yourself what date, 1,2 or 3 years out in the future. If your goal is to win a Grammy then define that time frame 1,2 or 5 years from now. Believe me this is not an open-ended deal. Time is ticking and before you know it the Grand Daddy of all "Dream

Stealers" will be knocking at the door, and that will be "Personal Responsibility." I assure you it will make its way into your life sooner or later.

If it is your goal to "Become the Idol" you should embrace and use all the forces around you to define your true direction and get to work. Once you set that date then everything else you do moving forward should be invested in that plan and the success date.

Let's again use the scenario of the desire to win the Daytona 500 five years from now. First, it is most likely you may know something about racing already. Next, you will need a car, not just any car, a car that can win and a car that can compete against the leaders. Third, you need a crew and not just any crew the best crew. Finally, you need the dedication to spend the countless hours on the road running to race after race until you gain the attention of race fans, the media, news, investors and sponsors. Although at the beginning you may have the best-looking car, the loudest motor or have minor sponsors that makes you look like a winner but inside you have to have the desire to win.

You cannot be the winner in the music business until you can prove you can run upfront against the best of the best. It is again your responsibility. Be consistent and stay upfront, event after event until you are invited to the grand race. The same goes for the music and entertainment business.

I ask, why does one movie with a 5-million-dollar budget become a blockbuster while another movie with a fifty-million-dollar budget becomes a huge flop? It is not about the money spent, but rather the content, the individual performances of the artists and the lasting impression that is left so that the word of mouth affect take hold and drives the success. This is the equivalent of going "Viral" in the tradition marketplace. If you have a great looking car that sticks out better than the rest but is always bringing up the rear, then what's the purpose. No one cares much about those performers. Like in any competition there will be diehard fans of even the worst baseball team who have never won a championship. To make it to the world series and walk away with the title takes consistency, practice, sacrifice, dedication, creativity, an open mind and focus. Each of these attributes are necessary and even more so in the entertainment and music industry.

The artist or performing group that only practices one evening a week is not serious about making a successful career in this business. These organizations are generally hobbyist that do not understand or possess the focus and dedication it takes to make a solid impact. A professional athlete is drafted into the league of champions because of mastery of skill and also by being an asset to the club (the investor or record company).

Let us start here. First comes self-evaluation and being realistic with yourself. Do you really have what it takes? Do you have the time to invest? Do you love what you do so much that you are open to professional outside and brutal criticism? Are you so unique that your organization's existence clearly separates you from all the other artists in performance and entertainment value? If you truly believe this than half the battle has been won.

The truth is, you cannot be the band or performing group that lets the wind blow it around with no direction or predetermined direction. You need to set your sail the right way and stick to your course no matter what. Secondly, who are those other people you are sharing this journey with? Yes, your crew and your band mates. Are they the right people? Are they the right partners you need in attitude and talent that will survive the test by fire? Just like serious poker players, are they truly "ALL IN." If not, you might just quit while you are ahead. It only takes one bad egg to ruin your chances of success. This expedition must have a truly dedicated crew with the right skill set or the probability that the ship will end up on the bottom of the abyss is almost guaranteed. It does not matter how much you may like them or owe some loyalty. In this business, none of that matters. It is about calculated total success.

You need to have the support from the best players and dedicated entertainers as possible to execute flawless scripted creative spectacles. This is accomplished through dedicated proactive and creative intent. If you think you have all the answers and you are to cool and have everything covered then I guess you don't need anyone one else in your journey. Find out quickly if your band is infected with the "everyone does not understand us" virus or the "our music is what we stand for" bug. If so, then it is time to see a career doctor because the life expectancy of your organization is already on the decline.

Don't get me wrong, it is good to have a good "self-attitude" but please leave it at the door if you are going to be in this business for many years to come. You can survive this phase of climbing the ladder fast but it is only based on your ability to create true entertainment that people come back time after time to experience and support. Four artists dressed in bear suits playing great music and giving good entertainment that call themselves the "Bare It All's" have a better chance of getting booked for real money then the cookie cutter original bar band with the cool attitude. Why, because that is just the way it is … accept it. The journey up to great heights requires the right planning, preparation, attitude and support.

Chapter 29
You Need the FBD Factor

What is the FBD Factor? Simply:

The First, The Best or The Most Different.

After all these years managing, mentoring, coaching, pulling my hair out and watching and nurturing bands and artists, I have concluded there are three things that are the strongest attributes to making it in this business.

True sustained success comes at a minimum of one or more of the FBD factors. If a performing group can muster up all three key attributes the world is the limit. These attributes are:

1) You must be the FIRST to do it.
2) You have to be the BEST at what you do.
3) You have to be the most DIFFERENT.

What does "being the FIRST to do it" really mean? It means you need to have that new car smell. Something that sticks in your mind, a new dance move or style, new rhythm, new beat, something new new new new! If you decide to take this path, then do it! But when you do, be the best at the new creation you have brought to life. Make it entertainment worthy and make history. Make it yours in every way and form.

Your next option is to add another key attribute of "be the BEST at it." Twist it up into something "DIFFERENT" as well. This creates true marketability. OK, let's take the back seat out and load in all the stuff that does not work in this scenario. Let's think of what goes on in a hard rock club when it comes to the competing musical groups. Every band must have countless tattoos, same clothing and same hair, and almost the same music. Reminder, this same spectacle is played out every night thousands of times across the world. If there is not something uniquely different with one of the bands then everything becomes a big blurr.

Ask yourself and think about this carefully. Why is it that you remember one performance over the rest? Be honest with yourself. Is it because this special band or artist has at least one of the FBD attributes that they have perfected? Why is one rose picked out of the bunch? I call these sticker bands, ones that stick to your ribs for some reason. You only see the single red rose in the sea of white roses.

It is so easy for new unskilled or unproven bands to try to emulate their favorite idol bands but great bands and artists destined for stardom do not try to replicate or clone themselves into popularity. The goal is, you want other bands to try to clone your style, your new music, your pulse and magic.

Do you have the FDB factor? You need at least one factor but if you can work to engineer all three factors into your act then your chances of success is multiplied by 300%. To become successful, you must have something so excellent that that everyone wants to give you their money or wants to sponsor you. You want them to fight over your brand.

"Make entertainment, make it yours in every way and form"

Chapter 30
A Career Choice or Just for Fun

The simple truth is, you must do something right to last ten years in this business. Where are you in this regard? Do you just want to be a one hit wonder or keep sewing your wild oats for a couple more years? Do you want to keep whacking the ball up in the air until you get your fill? Do you want to keep chasing your dreams with no success for the next ten years or design a plan that will work for "YOU", NOW?

You must make an impact on the market or on someone else's pocket book to last in this business. You must not just do something but do it right. Following some of the basic rules is a good place to start. Given changes in technology, electronic distribution, social media, trends, timing and evolving music company business plans structures, we all must understand what was right ten years ago may not be what is right today. However, as we have discussed before, one thing that has not changed from years past is developing and defining "Good Entertainment Value" and supplying the fans with want they want today.

What is unique about the entertainment business is that the script can be changed on demand to fit the changing market trends and directions. If observed in a timely manner, your organization's direction can be redesigned and redirected on a moment's notice.

One big "Dream Stealer" for many artists is that they continue to beat a dead horse. Many bands write hundreds of songs without testing their efforts. Successful organizations test their product, survey their audiences, fans and focus groups to determine what material appeals to their given markets. We don't want to get into other areas of importance right now including: Visual appearance, branding, image or visual market design at this point. I will leave this for the next book. However, you need a fighting chance or the market will turn a blind eye to your expensive efforts if you don't know what will work out of the blocks.

We are all exposed on weekly basis to new bands, TV shows or even new movies trailers on mass media, internet and social media. They come in clever promotional clips and "tastes" of products. No different than going to a grocery store and being given a taste of a new imported frozen chocolate truffles in the frozen section. This works because if you get a taste of something good you might like it and give it a chance. That is why playing to new audiences and getting airplay exposure is so powerful. But always do it at the right time and when you are perfectly prepared. If you are just going to have fun with this and not venture off into the murky world of this business, then none of this applies. So just enjoy yourself. For most professional musicians, it ends up becoming a hobby later on but for those starting out you have to make your choice, a hobby or the stars.

It is the battle of the trailers out there. Good trailers can make or break a new movie, new product or even a new musical act. Nothing in this regard has changed in twenty years and the professional marketing and promotional people know it and you should as well. Those who resist this concept are destined to fail on a global scale and dissolve into the distant memory never to achieve the dream.

It takes extraordinary efforts by extraordinary people to achieve extraordinary results. The efforts needed to rise to the top in this industry is matched with the efforts needed to succeed in any career, entrepreneurial venture or business. The entertainment business is a bit different. This difference is related to developing "Entertainment Value" that we have already discussed many times in this book. Entertainment value is the sparkle. People buy diamonds based on their sparkle, clarity, lack of imperfections and shine.

Ask yourself how often do you practice your skills? How much time do you spend studying currently successful artists and performers? What magical combinations are other artists using that would work for you? Do you have a "REAL" success plan? Is your intent defined? If your band's "Success Plan" is to be the BEST cover band on the planet, then so be it. Then be the best cover band ever in every detail. If you do it right, you can be wildly successful. If it is your goal to write hit songs, then get to it. Quit dreaming about it.

It is most likely your first 100 attempts could fail miserably. You only can earn your black belt thru practice, and pushing your comfort zone. Don't be afraid or influenced not to try new things, or pushing your abilities to the limit. Express and exercise your opportunity to try.

There is a time to work and practice and a time to play and waste time. The truth to many artists is they just do not take this effort seriously and only spend an hour or two a week doing these things we are discussing here. Where would any successful track star, sports star, violinist, dancer, singer, writer, and actor be if they only practiced their craft causally? Without perfection through exercise they only become stand-ins for the real deal. They may all start the race but very few would be presented with the awards (fame and fortune) they deserve. They may not become popular or be presented endorsement agreements that make them wildly financially successful either. I suggest the success plan should only include the successful minded players who are willing to commit to the hard work, endure the hardships and exhibit the essence that will allow for nothing but total success. This may mean working without a missed beat or a safety net for 40 hours a week if that's what it takes.

This is a serious business with serious consequences of wasting valuable time and money (and in many cases others peoples time and money). Thomas Edison tried 20,000 times to bring together the right materials, process, people, current technology and knowledge to make the first light bulb. However, once he found the right combination history was made. If he had stopped at attempt 19,999 someone else with the resilience would have achieved the same results and benefitted.

Most successful ventures (artist or bands) need to embrace the concept of working 5-7 days a week pondering, redesigning, non-stop visualization, market education, improving skills, trying new things and taking "Risk" to a different creative level. Finally, "DO NOT PROCRASTINATE" yourself into the grave.

"It takes extraordinary efforts by extraordinary people to achieve extraordinary results"

Chapter 31
Where Is Your Imagination

Let's face it some people have it and most don't or are not willing to take the journey. Walt Disney had imagination, he built an entire industry on it. He empowered many others with imagination to create fantastic things. These are the products born from the process of the individuals that can stop and just dream a bit, visualize a little bit more and create from nothing unimaginable things. These creations and visions take on a life of their own, but there must be the willingness to proceed with creating value from nothing. It always has been a mystery to me why most musical artists trying to make it in the entertainment business don't grasp the concept of true artistic creation and simply become imitators and perpetuators of the same old thing. Huge success in the music business depends on NOT maintaining the status quo. If one takes the time to study the evolutionary success of the musical artist you will find all have their beginnings launched on something fresh, new and different. Everyone wants to see the oddity, the different and almost freakish talent.

If there was someone with a 7-octave range that would qualify them for the club or an eight-year-old on a TV talent contest that sings flawless opera like an adult. These talents started from somewhere through imitation, imagination or simple innocence. With lots of support, practice, dedication this club is destined to take center stage. Do not miss out on using the basic building blocks of the entertainment business and bettering your odds in making it to the levels you dream of.

Songwriting comes from the imagination, new audio recording techniques, new stage development visuals, new lighting effects, almost everything on TV and at the movies comes from someone's imagination. Our commercial world is powered and depends on imagination. Where is your imagination? Underdeveloped and underutilized? Don't have time for it? They've told you as a child don't play "make believe" because that is stupid. Are you to cool to wander from the path of conformance?

Please make sure you want to be in the entertainment business because if you do you need to press the limits, go to the edge, and take chances and journey to where imagination will take you. Forget your peer pressure variables, it's not anyone else's investment but your own.

Yes, you can change the course of an entire industry if you are willing to try new things and use your imagination. As an example, please consider this, why is a group of successful musicians that paint their faces blue and were latex body suits so successful on so many levels? Thousands of people every day pay small fortunes to be "Entertained" by this unique twist on music and performance. Don't you want audiences to leave your performance and say "That was crazy, WOW! They were so great! What a fantastic show!" Then why settle for less?

Do you have great songs or are they just, OK? Do they sound just like every other band? You simply cannot let this happen.

Hundreds of bands send me invitations to come see them. Unfortunately, I am usually 99.9% disappointed. When I get a chance to give professional advice I usually get the closed-minded road block look. I frequently ask, just to get a response "so where is your entertainment value and imagination?" We all know the answer to this one, don't we? How would you answer?

Anyway, back to the point I am driving here. Imagination is what makes a band or artist standout as one of the ultra-special artists. They purposely present the industry with something new and groundbreaking in content, presentation and performance. Each of these seeds are sprouted from imagination not replication, imitation or copying another's success. Following a specific style of music is fine but copying every move, attire and beat does not set you aside as unique. Break away learn how to imagine and make up your own experience.

Chapter 32
The Players, Power Brokers And the Pawns

Placing your future into someone else hands is surly the trap that can have serious consequences. This choice must be reserved for the similar trusts required by astronauts to the engineers, flight directors, technician, mechanics and the proven procedures that send them up on super explosive and dangerous rockets. Do you trust those around you in your career choice? Do you know who is telling you the truth and who truly has your best interest at heart? You better know.

I am going to focus on the perception that every artist needs help to make it to the next level of success. They need help on many levels. This is quite true since any success or failure by an artist has a residual effect on other people including any potential backer you may have.

So, what is the right path for an artist that is working so hard to break out? There are established organizations and connected individuals that CAN make a difference and CAN make or break an artist. These individuals for whatever reason have their hands on the industry pulse and possess tremendous influence. The goal of most artists should be to attract, meet and be recognized by these people. If an artist rightfully deserves this attention, then the chances are they will at least be evaluated at some time for their potential and future impact on the bottom line. Getting the opportunity to be placed before these people is somewhat a privilege and usually a one-shot deal.

The entertainment industry is an established locomotive moving down the tracks at a blazing speed. The train is the same but the cast of characters is constantly changing. New power brokers are constantly hopping on and off as the opportunities wiz by. The power people in the major companies change their seats as fast as the next hit song falls off the charts. This is not as true for the smaller major independent privately held companies that offer the rising artist some great alternatives to grow their organizations. They can offer other options that may not be possible with the major companies. The goal is to be recognized to the point that a lucrative career building relationship can be forged. This is certainly a good path to take but there are many other environments that may have the reverse affect.

I do consider my role in this business as an alternative to the general path most take on their quest to be recognized. I say this because there are countless others in the forest that seek to "Hook Up" with popular high potential artists and go on the ride. That is their goal. They are not artists, writers or performers. They are business people, certified professionals or amateurs who are highly motivated to simply tell a great story to brighten the eyes of the budding artists. I wish I had a dime for every time I am asked to manage or promote a group. Most striving artists state they don't have the connections to take it to the next level. This always flattens me in wonder. The lesson here is if the band or artist has no "Entertainment Value" or unique commercially viable essence then it does not matter who I introduce them to. I am not willing to risk my reputation in asking for a power player's time to present the act. However, there are individuals that can talk a great story and are quick to bind a band or artist into a contract that surly will become problematic towards any artist's future.

Be careful here, many times a great band follows good advice and rehearses seven days a week and five hours a day until their show is a flawless spectacle. This band books a gig at a local concert venue and execute their show flawlessly only afterwards to be approached by a cast of characters (Producers, Managers and Attorneys, etc.) with business cards stating "You're the juice man, I can help you. I have connections and powerful friends, I know so and so and I can get you a deal." I say "Deal Smeal," Right? I do agree that some of these people are completely legitimate but the chances are against you. Your best asset is your amazing and flawless music and performance. This will attract the big fish eventually.

You need to be very smart who you accept into your club. You must and I repeat, you must do your due diligence before you decide to bring anyone from the industry onto your ship. If you don't, you most likely will find yourself signing a restrictive contract and paying retainers that make no sense at all. Someone will be selling you a map to gold fields that don't exist. The only person who can help you is yourself. Try following the things we have discussed in this book for starters.

As I mentioned in one of my previous chapters each band and artist needs to ask a huge question. Are you really at a point in your career where you need an attorney, sign with a manager or hire a promoter for a share of the cookie jar? Everyone wants your cookies. Are you so busy that you need someone to manage your business or read all the contracts being thrown at you? If not, wake up. If your band or the artist is so good, uniquely prepared and destined for success the power brokers will find you because you make yourself visible. By preparing your act so thoroughly you become a target.

Let me share one of my real-life experiences as a professional manager in regards to dealing with powerful established legal entities. I had the opportunity and privilege to discover and represent a freakishly talented artist. I decided to play one of my well-earned aces and bump them up to a proven industry legal entity that was one of those powerfully connected individuals we speak about in this chapter. After requesting a formal meeting in his office and after a four hour plane ride that day I was surprised to get his personal attention. After my dog and pony show this person commented "I can get behind this band, you have me on board." This was very exciting at the moment. However, in two days I get a communication on how excited this firm was and knows this was going to be a shoe in with the biggies that he represented. The reality is, he did have the connections and major relationships. Then came the sinker. Please send $25,000.00 and a rider for 15% before we will lift a finger to take this act into our big commercial clients. I remind you this came from a good friend of 15 years in the business.

If you want to play in this business, you may find yourself making some very difficult decisions if you want to take that route. I have no doubt, if the artist had in fact paid the fees than the artist would have been presented to the right individuals. When presented with this situation the artist was unable to commit. Therefore, the fuse was not lit from that end. There were no guarantees that the fees would do anything. We decided 25K could go a long way in self-promotion.

These situations are all over the industry and the budding artist needs to be careful and revert to their business plan for some sanity. The reality is, the road is hard. The easy road is paved with everyone with their hand out. If you don't have Solomon's fortune then you must rely on the sheer guts necessary to attract a team if individuals that can be honest with you and do what is necessary to open the doors to the powerbrokers themselves.

The secret is "make friends and build your industry relationships the old fashion way." If an artist's goal is to become successful in the commercial industry involving big establish companies and investors, then it is the artist's ultimate goal to make Mr. Big richer. By doing this you become wealthy and can achieve your goal of making a sustained living in the music business.

This scenario we discussed does not apply to reality competition TV shows that on occasion propagates a superstar. For those who go that route need to understand that the show's producers will require everyone to sign their rights away before the competition. This solidifies the deal in the event an artist happens to stick with the public and a superstar is born. The other alternative is to do it alone, create your own brand, use current accessible technologies, build your future one fan at a time and build a complete business out of nothing. Many have done it in the past and anyone can do it too. You will know when the time is right to assemble your dream team. Make sure you do it at the right time with the right people.

Chapter 33
Patience Please

Nothing of great value happens overnight, especially in the entertainment business. What's the hurry? Like anything in life, most want to see their desires to be rewarded immediately. Everything in the music and entertainment industry takes time. It is modification dependent, revision oriented and continuous risk taking is the norm. These efforts can be very expensive in time and treasure. Therefore, slow down the expectations and get to the work of working on what "will work" for you. If you are to be in the business of building a long term established career that will last, then this should be the goal. There are countless stories of wildly successful musical and entertainment artists that evolved countless times, changed market direction, took additional risks and changed up like a switch hitter to finally hit the winning home run. Writing that magical "Hit "can be done by design or through opening your mind and showing patience.

One of the most successful bands in recent history chose to re-record a hit from the past in their own style and was able to get the attention they needed to get some merited recognition. This band had it all, creativity, looks, uniqueness, musicianship and market appeal. After a few months, the track lost momentum and the band slipped away into the fog of all the next up and comers. The band shortly thereafter dissolved and two of the key members retreated to write a new album with a new band name. They spent months writing and recording a new album exploring new technologies, sound and researched new markets. When the new album was released, it did not gain much momentum or establish traction. Although intelligently written, the musicianship was exceptional and timely. The market acceptance was marginal and was not a good investment for the major players or industry commercial investors. Once again, the band retreated into the studio to work on a new approach to their music. They applied what they learned from their previous efforts and continued to experiment with new instrumentation and recording techniques. This again took months. The goal was to create something that worked commercially and was perfect for the time.

This band released a single from that effort and the rest was history, hitting # 1. They became a huge success worldwide.

A commercial success is created from a commercial product that is successful. It really is about what the public wants not what you want. It does not matter in what music style it is, it must be designed and cleverly created to have the expected commercial affect. This could take months or even years in some cases.

Any organized group should do their homework and pay attention to the success of other similar artists and experiment with new approaches to the same problem that others face in the effort to break through. Remind yourself there are thousands of other artists and bands with the same desires, dreams and goals as yours. Only the strong survive this business, only the focused and deliberate are entitled to keep their seat on the train of success. Only the givers can survive the test of time long enough to establish a long and fruitful career. When I used the term "Givers", I am speaking about those who want to entertain and be true to their skills and share their talent with others. They also show solid patience to achieve excellence.

The humble musician or performing group that gives of themselves before anything else get paid in dividends. There are millions of people worldwide that are open to great new ideas in music and entertainment just waiting to share their money with you. It is the patience that it takes to try whatever to meet each and every one of them that changes the course of the future.

It is a proven fact that most bands that withstand the tortures of touring, traveling, being away from home for endless days have an exponential better chance of success. It is also a fact that a certain amount of exposure through other means and media can also have a positive effect that can help the chances of success. Unfortunately, this usually comes with a financial investment that most up-and-comers generally cannot afford. This usually comes to a price tag that only major corporations or investors are willing to pursue and risk. If these individuals are willing to take the risk, then there are certain freedoms that also need to be given up for the opportunity. You must respect and have patience with these people.

Most artists and bands kick and scream all the way to the bank at the thought of perhaps having to do some of the things these major investors require. The biggest complaint is the perception of losing artistic freedom. Please, it is a two-way street here, a partnership, a coalition and friendship to share and bring each other's best resources to work on the battle and survive. It takes patience to work with other people and organizations. It takes effort to try to understand the other sides perception and respect the others involvement because they do have an investment and something to lose.

When an artist retreats to a safe place to create and work, it's just the beginning of the ultimate goal of commercial success. Bringing to the market the absolute best effort takes time and with painstaking efforts can make all the difference in the world. If creating the right vehicle takes years, then so be it. You must involve others in the journey and respect those relationships. They too have invested many years into their goals of providing the best entertainment that is to be offered.

It is a common thread that is connected to all artists. It is the voice deep inside that drives the artist and gives strength to pursue the effort. The skill to overcome any outside influence and push back the countless obstacles that the journey will surly expose along the way is the key. To some, it comes natural but to most it can be learned and properly applied. Listen to your coaches, mentors and others who have taken the journey before you. I assure you that if you are lucky enough to achieve a level of stellar success you will have countless people around you that will continue to influence the success of your career. Start now in developing those relationships with trust, honesty, patience and sincerity.

What goes up will come down if your business is not built on maintaining and respecting others investment in you. Believe me, in this business you are replaceable. Your focus on your attitude towards your journey can change the outcome at any given moment. Please define "Why" you are doing this. Do you have the patience for it? Is it because you love music so much that you want to be immersed in it all the time? Is it that you want to influence others in a positive manner? Is it your artistic expression that you can use to fund your future or just to share with others? What is the purpose of your efforts? If you know the purpose then it creates a sense of direction and defines your urgency. Remember this, if you are impatient you can become reckless with your future and can be perceived as unstable with the people who are driving and investing in your future. This includes your bandmates and other creative people around you as well.

Chapter 34
The Lasting Presence Will be Built in the Digital World

In the not so distant past it was truly impossible for the average individual to achieve forward movement in this business unless you owned a national broadcasting network (TV or RADIO) system or you where rich. If you did not own a major network, you certainly would have had to pay a King's ransom to access it. It would have taken all the rent money and college tuition at which to have the privilege to pay for access. This includes radio, magazine and other promotional tools. If you did not have large money support when the money was gone then so were you. Hence, no more presence.

Today an artist or band can have an ongoing presence on the internet through internet video channels, websites, direct feeds though social media networking and powerful mobile applications. The problem is, most fall short when they do not create entertainment value content that is worth keeping the attention of their fans or new viewers. It really is a one-shot deal with most when trying to keep a random or new fan excited about the next move. Building presences is possible though proper engineering for a designed affect.

The magic of the digital world today is that everything you do is instantaneous. Your effort can be transmitted around the globe in micro seconds. If you have an international following that you have built, then communication with your fans is priceless. The limiting step is that you must meaningfully communicate with your fans. Some new up and coming artists upload every little thing to the internet or video service. This can have a negative effect. You have a choice to hand feed the best of what you are creating to keep their interest. Why send out draft cuts of new songs or baseless videos? Think about or ask your fans what they want from you. Remember, you are building your future. If you want to include your audience and fans into your video diary then do so, but give them a reason to participate in it.

There are amazing people working in the internet world. Many are very talented programmers and visual artists. Get them involved, utilize all the tools, create great interactive websites and unique communication experiences and sponsor video conferences. All bands and artists need to utilize and learn about every digital promotional tool available to them. This is the future. Really, it's about that little TV in everyone's pocket. Closely watch two and three-year-old children, they can operate and select desired content with ease on iPADs and cell phones. Today's tablets are in every kindergarten classroom. This technology is burning itself into the fabric of everyone. All budding artists trying to make a mark on the industry need to learn and control this phenomenon for their own survival and benefit. The music industry also has taken it's time to understand how to utilize these powerful outlets to maximize digital music sales and generate substantial revenues worthy of its efforts and investments.

History shows theatrical musical live performance changed with the invent of local radio. Local radio changed with the introduction of broadcast TV that reintroduced live performance. Broadcast TV was made obsolete and was supplemented by cable, on-demand and satellite TV. Cable and Satellite TV was supplemented by the Internet. The internet then provided freedom of fingertip social choices and cellular mobile internet content. This technology released the constraints of the imagination and individualized communication over the entire planet. Just look around, it is a different world than it was 10 years ago. Obsolescence is the norm in technology. Digital socialization and communication will provide the future with an endless new set of variables. What is next? Keep your eyes open. Become the master of this technology and learn how to use it to your advantage.

Chapter 35
The Future In Music

I wish I had a dollar for every time I have been asked to predict the future of the music industry. As if I had a crystal ball or E.S.P. However, there is something special about those requests. I would not be doing my job if I did not project myself to where my natural abilities and experience can help provide probabilities based on common sense and awareness.

Recently while flying over the Midwest, I could see the lights of a major city of perhaps 100,000 people. I wish it was that easy to expose a new artist or band to that many people all at once. There is a huge world out there and artists must think this way. It is not about local successes now. The world is the market. The music industry has evolved into a whole new world with endless opportunities for those who can see and educate themselves about the new emerging technologies that can reach every person on the earth.

I would like to share my vision and premonition about the music business over the next 20 years. I believe, the choices will be limitless. Artists will control 100% of their own destiny. The record companies will morph into strategic partners becoming capital venture organizations feasting upon the cleaver artistic minds and tapping into their intellectual property pipelines. This is like hungry mosquitos on a summer evening looking for an easy meal. On the other hand, those who have the right approach using the technology available to them today and implementing cleaver business building will create a multimillion dollar business and wildly influence the industry right from their homes.

Those who do not embrace and educate themselves on the power tools of digital technology that are at their fingertip today will miss out on the greatest opportunities of the future.

Chapter 36
To the World, You Really Are A Superhero

Why do Super Heroes wear costumes? Why do police officers wear uniforms? Why do doctors and nurses dress the way they do? Why do pilots wear flight jackets, ties and hats? Because that is what separates them from the average public and assures their uniqueness and responsibility. It also identifies them as a professional that deserves respect and special consideration.

Why is it that professional entertainers must learn this fundamental behavior and attribute? The answer to this is that it corrects and focuses the artist state of mind to the task at hand. It is the effect artists have on those that are expecting the separation from ordinary to celebrity status that counts. That is why most successful artists dress, act and try whatever they can to stick out or be identifiable to the average citizen while in public or performing. The ordinary person is no different until they put on their super hero costume. When they do it makes them different, it makes their special talents stick out and makes them more entertaining. Like it or not that is how the public is programmed.

Most super successful artists easily tap into this concept and use it effectively. All budding artists should pay attention to this. One "Dream Stealer" is budding artists have a responsibility to create this affect everywhere they go or perform. If they don't they are missing the point. Why they generally try to deliberately separate themselves from the professionals make no sense at all.

The general buying public have a perception of what a successful artist should look and act like. The artist should also know that when it is time to do their thing that something must change about their personal attire, attitude and characteristics. To an artist's fan, the artist is bigger than life. They may even look at them as a superhero. With the wave of the artists hand the artist can make the crowd scream or jump up and down. On stage, they can be awash in bright lights and thundering sound to complement the illusion. That is just the way it works.

The upcoming artist should start to think about what separates them from the general bag of new competing performers. Many do and I am impressed when I see some artists go out on this limb to appear to have an individual identity worked out including attire and persona. This is essential in building a brand. This is the show business it's part of the make-believe world. All upcoming bands should attract or consult with talented people who know how to create this effect on the public perceptions.

I went to a club one evening in San Jose to watch a battle of the bands. Throughout the evening each band got on the stage and they all looked and acted like they all came off the same bus. There was nothing unique about any group musically or visually. Sure, there was some decent music played but no band stuck out. However, at the end of the night the last band had obviously explored the points of this discussion. When they came on stage they looked well prepared, nicely dressed in stage like attire, acted, and preformed accordingly. The audience also sparked up showing their delight for their efforts. This band exquisitely separated themselves from all others in the competition. I can still remember this band but not the previous seven bands. I do know that they won the competition.

It is a proven fact that stage performance is an art form worthy of effort and intent. It is a make or break situation for many musical organizations. Artists cannot avoid exploring this very important part of their responsibility to become popular and memorable.

It is amazing the push back I have gotten over the years trying to work with artists on this essential brand building concept. For some reason, most stick their fingers in their ears and hum a tune. The most offered response from unknown new artists and bands are "we like our image, we like our stage presence and we are who we are so we can identify with our fans." Oh, please let me chew on glass. This is not the right attitude or maturity needed to make it in this business. New artists need to be different, the best and the first to do something. This is true even if they must put on the right superhero persona to do it. A class act is a class act no matter how you look it and all artists need to be open to becoming part of the entertainer family. I am not going to consult you on how you accomplish this, it is up to you. Just be open to the possibilities for your future benefit. Do a good job making yourself memorable in all aspects of the art.

"Artists cannot avoid exploring how to become popular and memorable"

Chapter 37
Don't Underestimate The Power of Live performance

Countless emerging artists try to become successful by becoming recording artists before developing their live performance skills. Certainly, there is a place for artists to create and transfer their ideas to the recording medium. Unfortunately, not developing good live performance skills can derail a high potential artist and band in no time.

Live performance is a learned skill. This is the stuff that again turns new audiences into long term fans. Some have this natural live performance gift but most do not. There are recording artists that could care less if they ever play live. But if the artist's music grows wings then live performance will surely become extremely important. If one is trying to become a champion bodybuilder, then all the muscles need to be developed. If only the arm muscles are developed to magnificence and development of the legs is minimal then this defeats the effort in the competitive arena altogether. That's right, "Competitive Arena."

Remember this book is about trying to become the next new IDOL so your chances are magnified greatly if both recording and live performance skills are mastered. The goal of any artist is to be able to live the entire experience to its fullest and get everything out of the musical journey that they can.

Therefore, adequate time must be invested in developing and perfecting the artist's live performance to a point that it is executed flawlessly. Everyone on the team must operate as a well-oiled machine. This is expected of the artist when your audience pays hard earned money to see you live. If the performance is memorable then the residual affect will bring you one step closer to ultimate goal of becoming an established artist.

If you are a serious artist that wants to eventually become a signed major artist then there will come a time when you will be evaluated for all the skills. Therefore, it is to your best advantage to give the reviewer something to remember. The power of the live performance is undeniable. Don't cut yourself short and not make this process part of your regular rehearsal schedule.

When the recordings are done, it is time to put the frosting on the cake. If you need help to develop a great show then hire someone that can give you that edge or use your creative focus.

We will leave this subject out on the table for right now. You all know what I am talking about. Therefore, going into the specific skills and the techniques of live stage performance is a huge subject itself and we will leave it for the next book in the series. The point is, don't bore your potential new fans to death with meaningless antics and thoughtless visuals. Believe me, they are watching very closely. Especially after you have hooked them with your music and now they want to validate you as the "Real Deal."

> "Everyone on the team must operate
> as a well-oiled machine"

Chapter 38
There Is Room for One More In the Digital World

Example after example of monumental successes in the music arena surface each day even in these uncertain times

Exceptional rare and remarkable talents when properly applied can produce revenues that are equivalent to many top 500 Companies in a relatively short time. The digital world is a gold mine for the hard working and dedicated artist. It is a commodity based system that clever artists can use to open new markets throughout the world. Let us not forget the top line, proven and older artists that perhaps have already achieved stellar successes in today's music industry. They now have new business opportunities in the digital world that resurrects new beginnings.

The change in the music industry from an audio world to a visual world now requires artists to engage in creative exploration of new digital distribution techniques. Artist now need to evolve at the speed and demands of an extremely diverse consumer base. All artists must learn at all cost the new world around them and use all the technologies that are producing results. If one wants to become a "Bonified Idol," currently this knowledge gathering and mastering the internet must be at the top of the list. If required a digital content guru should be hired who can perform and guide your organization to massive exposure in cyberspace.

All the new artists of today are lucky that they have this asset available to them and the door is wide open now and for those creative enough to take advantage of the opportunity. There is plenty a space available for everyone. All the claims have not been taken.

"The digital world is a gold mine for the hard working and dedicated artist"

Chapter 39
Your Slice of The Rainbow

A rainbow can be a representation of the entertainment and music industry if one looks closely enough. If you look at a rainbow there are distinct colors, red, green, blue, yellow, etc. If we can together draw a comparison in regards to the music business, then the mind can be opened to what and how our eyes perceive and ears attract a certain type of music. We did touch on this subject a bit earlier but let's drive this point home now.

Let us take for instance the red color of the rainbow. Red could represent country music, perhaps blue urban rap, and green rock music. Why is it that when people see a rainbow it is such a mutually enlightening experience? Because it is just white light split into its individual parts. Just like music, each style is split clearly into its individual style. Let's take the green color as an example. In the rainbow if you expand the color green it is clear that there are many shades of green just like there are many different shades of red, blue and yellow. Let's look at the basic color green, it's sub parts can be lime green- which could represent soft rock, dark forest green, - heavy rock, grass green – classic rock. The red color could represent country music its subparts could be pink that could represent - country rock, light red - blue grass, dark red - traditional country. etc. Everyone prefers a certain color more than another. Everyone has their favorite style. You personally may only prefer County, Rock or Rap and could care less about the other parts or subparts.

In the United States alone there are approximately 300 Million people. A successful act is considered hitting the big time when they sell 500,000 or 1,000,000 nationwide. That is one in 300 people that buys an album of songs. To achieve a platinum record only 1 in 600 people would need to buy the product and 1 in 1,200 for a gold record. Remember albums are sold worldwide and it is a big world out there. Therefore, to achieve a gold or platinum record, this can potentially translate to 1 in 1000, 5000 or 10,000 or more. Get the message, you can't play music for everyone. Pick a color and stick with it, perfect it, own it and then become the color you choose.

Let's take these statistics and apply them to a different model. If you pass out 100,000 fliers to a concert and you use the statistics of 1 in 600 people will actually come to your concert. Than that would mean 160 people should come to the show for a given color of music. This is not out of line with the path to a gold or platinum record. Same goes with radio exposure. Enough radio stations broadcasting your music will generate a specific response you are expecting.

Each color has its own audience. Therefore focus on that slice of the market and don't try to please everyone else. There are many huge stars in every color of the rainbow and there are thousands of colors to choose from in the world arena. Stick to your color, perfect it.

"Get Your Slice of The Rainbow"

Chapter 40
A Very Touchy But Important Subject

Please let me discuss this topic without being branded as some sort of self-centered, disrespectful disconnected individual. I cannot tell you how many times (I've lost count) that I have been contacted by parents who believe their son or daughter is the next biggest thing. I mean this sarcastically, although I respect the efforts and belief parents have in their children but there can be a limit to their participation. The fact is, most parents know nothing at all about the entertainment business. Unfortunately, even though their knowledge may be limited they still find it a parental right to dictate and influence every minute detail of the young artist's musical journey. This simple action can be one of the biggest "Dream Stealers" of all and ranks right up there with the top shelf winners for budding new young artists. What confuses me is why they contact me in the first place. I believe it is just another opportunity for them to share their excitement and power over the situation.

The confusion lies when the parents tries to help the young artist and deliberately force their influence over the outcome for what "they" want for the young artist. Believe me, this can also happen with inexperienced managers who are trying to help a new artist. Hovering over every detail can become a detriment and can destroy the individualism, creativity and emotional stability of young budding artist. Unfortunately, it creates what I call "the over-coached artist or child." This is not true for all cases but does and will affect many in the negative way.

The only thing that has a long term positive affect on is encouragement. However, if the parent is willing to participate in a constructive and cooperative manner with the professionals to whom they are trying to involve, then this can become a win-win situation for the young artists and parent. So many times I have watched when some of the most promising and talented future superstars turn 18-year-old and completely walk away from an almost guaranteed successful career. This is because they have had enough of being told what to do every minute of their life and how to do it. You've all seen it.

Although the parent's intentions are good, the dynamic of a creative artist (young or otherwise) phycology cannot be taken for face value. It must be understood for how that gift is influencing the emerging talent. People who have not been blessed with talent cannot understand how that affects the individual who must deal with the urges and drive that it creates internally. Young artist daydream on seeing themselves on the big stage. It may not be the same vision the parent sees. In some case these relationships are fruitful but only if the motivating parent understands the process and pitfalls associated with the journey.

The parent segregate manager should assess their own talents and experience in this business and be honest with themselves before attempting to influence the young talent. Wherever possible, if a unique talent is emerging early in life seek out and work with professionals and the likely hood of success will be much better.

"Young artist daydream, let them imagine the possibilities"

Chapter 41
The Ten Steps to Breaking Through to the Other Side

This chapter comes from the heart. I was once asked by a very talented new artist, "What do I need to do to get into the music and entertainment business?" Back then I never thought of this subject much. I was on cruise control and just moving forward with my projects. However, I did stop to reflect on my 30 years in this business and gathered my thoughts to offer the artist some solid advice. As I look back now I am grateful for his question.

Therefore readers, please consider the following ten steps that I identified that should help your chances in achieving a solid foundation for a potential career in this business. However, you must add you own creativity and vision:

"Success is a state of mind. This simple notion gives life to things that would remain in the world of the unknown. Like the universe the mysteries are yet to be discovered. In the entertainment universe, only the imagination can bring to life magical performances if created for a purpose,"   Jay Jaworski

Therefore, consider the following:

1. Define Your Purpose:

Ask yourself a question, why would someone want to have a life in this business with its ups and downs, stiff competition and massive odds against sustained success? The answer is in the natural DNA that all artists share for the love of creativity and the love of music itself. The difference is made when real purpose is added to the mixture. Nothing is wrong with becoming financially successful, this is a good purpose. Without financial success in any business the life expectancy of any venture is limited. Do you just love to create and express your philosophy on life and love? That is a good purpose. How about creating music that inspires others through difficult times or you just want to simply "entertain, entertain, and entertain some more?" These examples are also great purposes, what is your purpose? Once you have figured that out then the next step is a natural flow that just leaks out. Does it matter? Yes, it certainly does matters! Ask any successful artist, musician or band and you will get a very clear answer, "It's what I (we) do, it's my (our) purpose in life."

To "Become an Idol" you must make it a priority to affect scores of people in such ways that it fulfils your purpose. On the other hand, if you want to use your creativity and art to feed the world then make that your purpose. What is the purpose of obtaining a medical degree? To help people regardless of the monetary rewards or driven only by the money and not sincerely care about the people? The music business has similar motivations but it is driven by satisfying the audience and fans first. Do you only care about yourself or the affect you would have on others? Think about it. Purpose gives you a reason to focus which drives your efforts. Purpose goes hand and hand with a unique and special attitude.

2. <u>Be Realistic and Be Honest with Yourself:</u>

You must do a complete assessment of yourself. Do you believe you have what it takes to go the distance and have the burning desire to succeed? Mostly, do you truly believe you have the talent required to make your efforts worth spending valuable time chasing around a dream in a dark room filled with unseen obstacles? These are very hard life changing decisions that have to be made.

Everyone is born with unique abilities although we can sometimes see other things about ourselves that we wish we could accomplish. A music and entertainment career has a very defined life cycle, a beginning, middle, end and sometimes an afterlife effect. This life cycle generally lasts about 2-3 years if the right chain of events is assembled to allow the process to begin. Be honest with yourself, are you willing to meaningfully invest 2-3 years of your life dedicated to finishing what you started? Many who have gotten their feet wet in the trial and error process begin to sense the life cycle affect with each passing day. Regardless and for some reason continue with the belief that their big break is just over the next hill and keep going.

If progress is not being made and if it is not measurable then be honest with yourself and try a different approach. The different approach you may take could be radical in nature but could be exactly what you are looking for. As my successful musician father shared with me long ago "if you need a helping hand you will only find it at the end of your right arm." The real help comes from being honest with yourself. Quit fighting the reality and focus on your purpose, get the right attitude, be honest with yourself and quit wasting time. Nothing comes easy. To become an elite, you must join and accept the rules of the club. Certainly, having a special talent helps but sticking to the plan and getting it done give you a chance. Quit procrastinating and believe in yourself. Always remember this is the entertainment business so create "True Entertainment Value."

3. **Fix Your Attitude**

You have a powerful gift in your tool box and that is your attitude. Your attitude effects everything. When applied to the entertainment industry a clear winner attitude is the catalyst of creativity. Someone with a bad attitude about the music business will end up on the cutting room floor because the music and entertainment business is a positive process.

I can hear a bad attitude from across the street. Sounds like: I'm not good enough, I will never make it, I don't have enough money, I don't know anyone, I don't have the confidence of others. If this is your world, then your attitude is worthless to you. Stop, stand up and get excited about your ability to dream. Smile and get excited about living.

An incredibly good attitude will surely become infectious to others including audiences. Someone with a great attitude regardless of the things that may be blocking their way can overcome all obstacles. Your attitude comes through loud and clear in your art, body language and music. Don't fool yourself, others have a keen ability to read it. If you believe you are going to measure up to others in your musical or entertainment world, then your goal is to excel in your attitude and become an example which will fuel your success.

4. **Get to Work on Your Plan:**

When you go on any journey there has to be common sense built into the effort. This business is no different. Every building, vehicle or product when through a process to be created. The quality of the final version is a direct reflection on the thoroughness of planning and the attention to the details. Same goes with rock stars.

You have to begin here. You have to work through it. Anyone who thinks otherwise is just fooling themselves. How many times have you heard an album of songs that had one song that was exceptional while the rest of the tracks were weak leaving no lasting impression and leaves you unsatisfied? I call those "filler songs" and nobody likes an album full of filler songs. What would be a stage dancing group who used the same moves time after time for 10 songs only to change their costumes? The secret to longevity and repeatability is no different than the magic created in a huge Las Vegas theatrical spectacle. It is designed from the beginning to become just that, a "Spectacle" that has the endurance to last years. Throwing together 10 songs with mediocre players and throw it out there is not going past the home plate in this world today. Your plan of success is imperative. All the parts and pieces must fit together perfectly.

5. **Do your Research:**

You must ask the important questions to understand your place in time. Here are a few to get the juices flowing: What are fourteen-year-old girls getting excited about these days in regards to new music? What are 18-25-year-old men spending their money on?

What are 25-40 year women spending their money on? What concerts are packing them in? What videos are going viral? What bands and artists are signing up millions on social networking? There must be a thousand other questions you can ponder. The answers to the questions you ask will have a bearing in your potential plan. Ask yourself these very important questions and then revise and update your plan to the best effort possible. If you don't know where you are going or even if there may be water along your journey why even attempt to take up the challenge. If you do not know how social media works then admit it and find a Guru who does. Someone must find the answers, the talent, the songs, the look, the right direction and the right approach, and so on.

Many artists claim that they need help to get the interest they deserve. Why would anyone go into any commercial effort or business venture without the right knowledge to take advantage of a void or fad? Building a solid and impressive career is the objective, it does not fall out of the sky. If one wanted to become a competitive body builder it would take knowing and understanding the established rules and efforts required to achieve the high level success to compete. How long and how much time to invest in the effort? What is the commitment? Part of the plan for making it in this business is to seek and locate expert advice, mentoring and coaching. Don't be afraid or be so self-reliant to a fault that you don't ask for honest help. This is a huge mistake.

6. <u>Practice Makes Perfect</u>

Most artists and bands don't understand that the music and entertainment business is a job. Your efforts should be a full-time commitment. This commitment should have established milestones that must be met. These milestones are directly and carefully created from the plan. Are you willing to do the work necessary? If not visit the job board down at the college.

Schedule everything you do around a defined time table. Your practice time is deadly serious business. No different than a pro sports team, ballet dancer or race car driver. Musicians and bands are no different. These practice sessions are to be designed to press the limits so that when the curtain opens on your future career your performance is executed flawlessly. This is not a party, although most artists seem to disagree but give it about two years and a little bit of water under the bridge and the reality will set in and the party will be over.

Any artist or group of artists have the power at the tips of their fingers. But they must laser beam focus all their resources and efforts into a work of massive value. The flaws cannot be ignored. They must be corrected and lined up to vibrate in such a way it will make history for them. That only come with real practice.

What is Practice? **PRACTICE** = **P**erformed **R**aw **A**t **C**reation, **T**ransformed **I**nto **C**reative **E**xcellence.

Serious practice is like air or money if you don't have either one you will always struggle. This goes for all artists, beginners or seasoned professionals each must without question take practice seriously or the watering holes will dry up and the future just dies. Practice with intent, push the limits, step out of your comfort zone a little at a time. How bad do you want the rewards for your hard work? Successful organizations practice 5 or 6 days a week because they are the champions and want to stay on top. Champions must work even harder than the competitors to maintain what they have worked so hard for.

Once you have perfected your skills to a level that you can just enjoy your efforts then look forward to that day when you look back and say I would not have changed a thing.

What is the flip side "I wish I would have worked harder on my dream?" If you don't take this step seriously then this is exactly what you will be saying to yourself someday.

Find a place to work. All artists need a creative studio and environment to exercise. Find a place that has the room to express yourself musically, physically and creatively. If the members of your organization are not with the program and cannot or will not commit to a solid rehearsal and practice schedule, then it is time to find those who can commit.

7. Run with the Right Pack

It cannot be stressed enough how important this is. You must choose the right partners, performers, players and business people. You must find players that have the same desires and similar goals that you do. At the beginning, all is fun and wonderful. As in all relationships, if common respect, trust and solid attitudes toward success is not present then the relationship will end. This will result in mounds of wasted time, dreams and money that will be swept from the floor of the studio and the "Dream Stealers" will have won.

It does not matter if an artist or player or writer is the "Hottest" in the neighborhood or can perform beyond imagination. It is about being able to build a future for everyone involved, even if you personally think you are the "King" and the entire universe revolves around you. There is always time to humble yourself. Whether you like it or not others have and or will have time invested in your successful career. These people may turn out to be investors, supporters and even your fans. Also, managers, producers, players, roadies, writers, etc. Your organization should be a family unit that requires stability long enough to cash in.

Ask yourself, what skills are needed to participate in the success building process? What kind of a person do you need to develop? Are these the right people that you have chosen to spend your valuable creative years with? As an alternative example, successful movies are made by a very focused casting process and successful mega companies are built by the talent they obtain and retain. Most great feats of human accomplishments were not accomplished alone. Without a serous team building selection process disaster shall become the organization.

Ultimately in this business even a little bad review or failure to connect with your potential audience will choke future ticket sales and music sales. If the team is not on point the organization is subject to bad reviews. You cannot afford uncooperative members that fail to deliver 110% all the time towards the goals set. If this mismatch of cooperation of members occurs the death rattle sound will start to be heard. All it takes is one key person without the same goal and attitude including producers, managers and records company and the dream will fall like the eggs at the summer picnic egg toss.

It takes time to pick your friends and trusted business partners and creative collaborators as well. The human factor is the most difficult so handle so this step should be handled carefully. Remember to "Become the Idol" you must "Become" what you have planned to be. This plan must take into consideration others that also have a burning desire to achieve the same level of success. This can have a great side effect that creates long term and rewarding relationships. You most likely will spend countless days on the road with each other away from home so compatibility is essential. Therefore, find the right Band of Brothers or Sisters to journey with. This is supposed to be fun.

Lastly, everyone must be on fire about the processes and truly have a purpose or else disagreement will undermine the chances of success. Disagreement and separation happens to the best of them because sometimes people and musical groups lose focus on the true intentions of the organizations. Don't fall into this pit. The pit of "Dream Stealers" will rip you apart.

The keen leader of the organization should pay close attention to recognize the symptoms and correct them immediately before they become a cancer and kills the efforts. If changes need to be made, make them immediately so that you are replacing the critical mechanics that your rely upon. Plugging in the right component at the right time is essential so that the journey can continue and the organization is improved. If this happens and you believe you have been born on earth with all the talent, vision and divine blessing to become the next King of "X" then great. Just remember your future will involve many wonderful and dedicated people who will help you to that end. There must be some simplicity to the process to give it fun and time worthiness but not at the expense of your ultimate success or turning away valuable assets. Don't let the weeds strangles your growth toward success and achieve your goal of becoming an important part of the entertainment business because of a people problem. Find the right individuals to run with. They will be your family and your pack.

Personally, and on this note, I would take a solid and serious, dependable, open minded, humble band or artist over a self-proclaimed prodigy, self-destructive and closed minded artist or group at any time to invest my valuable time and hard earned money and you should also.

8. Make Your Commitment Stick and with Excellence

All success requires extreme commitment and dedication to finish what you started. Anything else is unacceptable if you want a career in the entertainment business. I know some of the most talented artists that are so committed that they will never give up. I respect this attitude. I like this thinking and have gained respect for them by watching them evolve into the fabric of this business.

If you want to go for the gold and "Become the Idol" you must make that same commitment. All the other talented people in your organization should also make the commitment to enter the race to win. If you are confident your race car can do the job and compete head on with the best of the best then believe in it and enter the race.

If you are not confident and committed to what you have created, then don't. Modify or build a new vehicle if that is what it takes. You have to be confident in your vehicle and only then you will have a winning chance.

It is fine to start over at any time if you have to, but start with a new approach and stay committed to the winner's circle. Most artists dabble in commitment and never go all in to win the tournament. Most don't take risks, don't go on adventures or journey off the path. Persistence will get the job done, commitment realizes the rewards. The reward is being able to make the transition into a career that you desire and always wanted from the beginning.

If the path of commitment is deviated upon then procrastination starts to set in and then it's all over. Time just keeps on ticking away, minute after minute while the procrastination bus just parks at the station. Bands, artists and performers give up to easy, don't make this mistake. Remember your plan, nothing is easy everything is difficult but stay true to your art and finish the story. What will be your story? think about it. You can write your own story. I ask you now, are you ready for this journey, really? Are you truly committed to live this life in the entertainment business? Then get on with it get off the procrastination bus, NOW!

Your commitment to excellence in your efforts to launch your rocket to the moon must be coupled with patience. So many artist and bands are so eager to have people hear their work they are willing to just throw little bits and pieces out into the public just to get a response or need a response to keep justifying their efforts. This is just silly. Remember your commitment should be to build something amazing.

So many artists upload marginal quality material as fast as they can finish a demo in their home studios so their limited number of followers can be satisfied. This behavior is not important to the business builder entertainment entity. This is like releasing one chapter of a book at a time. The commitment should be to finish the book. Once the creation is done it can be presented for it intended affect as a complete entertainment value effort. The commitment should be made to present the art in its fully prepared state. Even the most successful bands and artists must operate in this manner.

Therefore, get all your shows elements together, commit to rehearsing until you cannot rehearse any longer then rehearse some more. Get all the music ready and stick to the script playing it note by note, step by step, night after night, month after month until you get out what you wanted from your creation. Don't piece mail out your future and career.

You should also commit to creating at a minimum a one (1) hour show. It does not make sense to even spend money and effort to promote an artist that is not able to support the live performance requirements immediately. If a song is fortunate enough to go viral, or gets on the radio on normal rotation, the artist should be immediately ready to go for the gold. I highly recommend that when you do get a chance to play for your new fans you had better not disappoint them. As I've said before, your job is to make fans out of new audiences. Their first impression of you must be over the top. This also goes with posting videos on the internet. Don't put out inadequate material that does not meet your "break out standards." Your commitment should be to only provide what is of the finest quality and entertainment excellence.

9. Avoid the Dream Stealers

They are all around you, seen and unseen. Always pay attention to the road signs and caution lights on this journey. Don't let them into your life. Be smart, don't be careless. This is a business and it needs to be treated with respect if you expect it to take care of you in the future. Everything you do, every minute you invest, every temptation you follow, every person you meet has an influence on your future. The biggest "Dream Stealer" is time. Don't take time for granted, don't procrastinate and get to work, create and get it done.

10. Entertain, Entertain and Entertain Some More

Lastly, you're in the entertainment business plain and simple. Your job is to entertain your way to a wonderful experience, incredible memories, and a sustained fullness of your life. You must remember this one simple thing. Don't confuse entertainment with just going through the motions. All your efforts must be designed for the effect you want to obtain. This book offers some different perspectives on this issue that can be used to give you the edge to fulfill your dreams. Use them, every chance you can.

Chapter 42
Closing Words of Wisdom

I wrote this book for a purpose, the purpose to record the observations of my journeys throughout my career in the entertainment business. If you too were to take the time and write down your life's knowledge what would you write about? What can you say today about your current journey in the music industry? What would be the purpose to share that information and who would it be intended for? You may ponder even if you felt that the wisdom, experience and knowledge that you have in your possession even has any value. But what if you could share and inspire only one person in this world to achieve a dream, rise to their true potential and are able to grasp the blessing of their God given gifts. It would be well worth the effort. What if you could inspire one person out of millions?

So therefore, I wrote this book for that one person who wishes to listen, ponder, dream and take a journey into my world, see what I have seen, watched what I watched, experienced what I experienced. Learn from what I have shared in this book so that you can understand the journey, pitfalls, dangers, joys and the rewards that are so much desired to be part of this difficult yet rewarding business.

The entertainment and music business is magical and a blessing to all those who take the right path and dedicate themselves to mastering the craft. I wish you the best of success that you are able to achieve the level you dream of. Never let the "Dream Stealers" into your life. Make sure that everything you do is dedicated to becoming the best entertainer possible as those who have come before you. Never forget when you yourself "Become the Idol" help others to complete their journey and your destiny will have come full circle. If you help those other deserving talented people get what they dream, then you will have received the best that life can offer you. Never Forget:

> *"Be the absolute best at what you do, be different, be the first to do it and be true to your art. Trust the wisdom and learn from the explorers who have taken the journey before you and never forget that this is the Entertainment Business. Your job is to entertain your way to success and transport others to amazing places."*
>
> *Jay Jaworski*

Star Mentors Series

BECOMING THE IDOL

CustomerService@StarmentorsPublishing.com
www.StarMentorsPublishing.com
www.BecomingTheIdol.com